THE
HARD
COMMANDS
OF
JESUS

THE
HARD
COMMANDS
OF
JESUS

Roy Pearson

BAKER BOOK HOUSE
Grand Rapids, Michigan

THE
HARD
COMMANDS
OF
JESUS

Roy Pearson

BAKER BOOK HOUSE
Grand Rapids, Michigan

PHOTOLITHOPRINTED BY CUSHING - MALLOY, INC.
ANN ARBOR, MICHIGAN, UNITED STATES OF AMERICA
1976

FOR

BEVERLY

with the prayer
that finding the commands of Jesus hard,
she may not think them impossible

Preface

IT IS NOT A SIMPLE TASK TO CHOOSE "THE HARD COMMANDS OF JESUS." In one sense, none of his commandments is hard; for the gospel is the good news that in comradeship with Christ the yoke is always easy and the burden ever light. In another sense, however, all of his injunctions are hard; for the years have not disproved the claim that the gate is narrow and the way strait, and that those who find them are few.

Some of Jesus' commands are hard because we do not understand their meaning; others because, understanding them, we do not believe them; and still others because, believing them, we do not have the courage to obey them. Behind most of the stern requirements of the gospel message, however, is some unwanted and unwelcome task which confronts us as a moral imperative whose nature we see, whose importance we know, but whose burden we do not want to bear; and these chapters call attention to some of the more essential of these moral imperatives.

A quick glance at the table of contents will reveal to anyone that not all of the hard words of Jesus are included in this book. Omissions have been made, in part because of the exigencies of space, in part because of the author's personal preferences, and in even larger part because of the way in which so many of Jesus' commandments are distinct on the surface but intimately related when their deeper meanings are seriously probed. There is a close affinity between "Go, sell what you have" and "Do not lay up for yourselves

7

treasures on earth." The same city can be entered along a road labeled "Have faith in God" or along another marked "Ask, and it will be given you." And someone else might have chosen to approach the message of the cross through the command that the followers of Jesus be servants, or seek first God's kingdom, or love God with all of the heart, mind, soul, and strength.

It may be well to confess at once that these chapters are aimed primarily at laymen like those to whom the author ministered for eighteen years—intelligent men and women knowing something about the Christian faith but wanting to know much more, partially committed to the Christian life but hesitantly pushing themselves into ever deeper commitment. The book attempts to take up its stand where these people daily live and move and have their being, to interpret the timeless gospel in terms of their time, and to avoid the formal language of theology, which would be as incomprehensible to them as it would be awkward for the author.

Roy Pearson

Contents

Chapter 1

GO, SELL WHAT YOU HAVE

Go, sell what you have, and give to the poor, and you will have treasure in heaven; and come, follow me.   MARK 10:21

OF ALL THE STORIES ABOUT JESUS ONE OF THE BEST KNOWN IS THAT OF the man who asked him what he must do to inherit eternal life. "Keep the commandments," Jesus told him, and when the man said that he was already keeping them, Jesus gave him those words of counsel which the Christian world knows by heart. But at that saying the man's "countenance fell, and he went away sorrowful; for he had great possessions."

Writing about this story in *The Ministry of Jesus,* Charles Francis Whiston makes this comment: "In return for earthly, perishable treasure, Jesus offers heavenly, abiding riches. That offer the young man refused. The possessions of earth were so real and tangible; the things of heaven so ephemeral."

It is probably safe to assume that Jesus' demand that the man sell all of his possessions was a specific prescription meant to meet a particular need, but the requirement that those who followed him should not be in bondage to any material master was a universal provision of discipleship in his name. And that is one of the principal stumbling blocks of the Christian life. Earthly things always seem so visible, so enjoyable, and so effectual; and spiritual things often appear so imaginary, so troublesome, and so helpless. Having a reasonable amount of material possessions, you can buy a steak, build a house, impress your friends, or wage a war; but when you think about the things of the spirit, you know that you cannot eat love, keep out the rain with kindness, buy a mink coat with mercy, or shoot down an enemy plane with faith in God.

We can put our hands on earthly things. We can see them, stand on them, and hide behind them. But the soul is so slippery, and the spirit is so elusive, and heaven is so heavenly that even earnest Christians sometimes wonder whether all their faith is foolishness and all their struggle vain.

I

No thoughtful man ever fully escapes this dilemma, and the first step toward its solution is the recognition of the simple fact that heaven *is* heavenly. Earth can do some things which heaven cannot, and treating heaven and earth as if they ought to be identical in their assets is no more wise than trying to describe a swordfish and a radio without using different adjectives. If water is wet, it cannot be dry; if stones are hard, they cannot be soft; and if this is a tree, it cannot be a cat. Earth is earth, and heaven is heaven. Each has its own attributes, its own powers, and its own rewards; and expecting either to perform the functions of the other is like wondering why your cigarette lighter will not mow your lawn or being surprised that your overcoat does not have a carburetor.

II

In the second place, it needs to be remembered that any emphasis on the spiritual which attempts to scorn the material is a perversion of the Christian gospel. Christianity is not simply an otherworldly religion. In fact, there are few religions which could rightly claim to be so materialistic as Christianity. "In the beginning God created the heavens," but he also created "the earth," and looking back upon his work, God saw that it was good. Jesus came to men because God so loved "the world," and when God set out to reveal himself to men, "the Word became flesh and dwelt among us." Jesus himself was known as a gluttonous man and a winebibber,

12

and what he had to say about the birds of the air and the flowers of the field leaves little cause for doubt that he enjoyed the earthly things around him and counted them to be a part of God's plan for his people.

Thinking of the sudden burst of interest in the possibility of interplanetary travel, J. B. Priestley made the trenchant remark, "One world at a time, please." The impatience for heaven which some people display makes one think of a little boy who complains that the school committee will not graduate him from high school when he has not even entered kindergarten. Mountains and meadows, animals and flowers, houses and automobiles, offices and stores, stoves and hammers and dishes—the things of earth are the gifts of God, and spurning them is no better than the act of a child whose parents have given him a bright new bicycle for Christmas only to see him hurl it angrily down the cellar stairs because he did not want a bicycle that year: he wanted a battleship.

III

So heaven is different from earth and ought not to be judged by the same standards, and earth has its own assets and can never rightly be despised. But still facing the seeming frailty of spiritual values, we need to recall also that things are not always what they seem and that seeing is not always believing.

A table looks solid, but most of it is empty space. An electric cable looks cold and dead, but it carries the power which operates a great factory. The stick thrust into a pond looks bent, but it still is straight. On a desert you see mountains which do not exist; and thinking that you see a moving picture on your television screen, you really see no more than a fast-moving bright spot which covers the screen with lines of light for the slow-reacting eye to interpret as a picture.

There are sights which the human eye cannot see. There are sounds which the human ear cannot hear. And as our knowledge probes deeper and deeper into the universe around us, more and more clearly we see the vastness of our ignorance. Once we thought that our discoveries were almost at an end. What the universe was we were sure that we had determined, and what could happen and what could not happen we thought that we knew. But now suddenly our universe has been blown apart again, and we find that we live in the midst of forces which we did not even know existed. Miracles are far more credible today than they were thought to be a hundred years ago, and it is one of the clearest signs of intelligence to be sure that men always see through a glass and darkly, that the known is but a fractional part of the knowable, and that surprises wait around the corner for anyone who thinks that things are always what they seem or that seeing is always believing.

IV

When the mind is thus left open to the advent of undiscovered truth, we see that the claimed stability of earthly things is amazingly unstable. One day Washington Irving went to visit the tomb of Shakespeare at Stratford on Avon. The tomb was in the chancel of the church, he wrote, and the place was solemn and sepulchral. Tall elms waved before the pointed windows, and always there was the soft murmuring of the River Avon close beside the church's walls. A flat stone marked the spot where the bard was buried, and a few years earlier some laborers had been digging there to make an adjoining vault when suddenly the earth caved in, leaving a vacant space, almost like an arch, through which one might have reached into the actual grave of Shakespeare. No one presumed to meddle with the poet's remains, however, and the old sexton kept constant guard for two days until the second vault was finished and the connecting arch tightly sealed. "He told me," Irving wrote, "that he had made bold to look in at the hole, but could see neither coffin nor bones; nothing but dust."

Of course, it is scarcely strange that the old sexton could not find the real Shakespeare in that ancient tomb—the creator of *King Lear* and *Macbeth* and *Hamlet,* the maker of *Twelfth Night* and *The Taming of the Shrew* and *A Midsummer Night's Dream.* Even when life is in the body, the mind and soul are never visible to earthly eyes; and when the body dies, they are not made more so. But the fleshly remains of Shakespeare were gone too, the old sexton said. The body, the bones, even the clothes and the coffin—all of them had disappeared. Nothing but the dust remained, and it is only being sensible to remind ourselves that this marks the inevitable end of all that we can see or touch or taste or hear or smell. Disintegration, dissolution, dust.

In terms of earthly things, man's sufficiency is always insufficient, and his adequacy is always inadequate. He is at the mercy of everything from microbes to drunken drivers, from the mistakes of surgeons to the hatred of enemies, from accidents on the back stairs to atom bombs dropped from high-flying planes. No man ever escapes the death of his own body, and although many scientists still disagree about the form of the earth's destruction, there seems to be a considerable consensus that sooner or later the mountains will depart and the hills be removed and that the earth will serve no more as a dwelling place for man. If we stand on nothing but the earth, we stand upon a sinking ship; and if we have faith in nothing but the visible, we have faith in nothing but the transient. The apparent security of material things is only an illusion. They cannot answer man's most important questions. They cannot bear his heaviest burdens. They cannot heal his deepest hurts. And he who puts his faith in them does no more than put his trust in a "broken reed of a staff, which will pierce the hand of any man who leans on it."

V

But if a closer look reveals that the claimed stability of earthly things is illusory, it also shows us that the apparent frailty of the spiritual is equally deceptive. What will a man not do because he loves his wife? Or what sacrifice is too great if a child's life is in danger? Or to what heights have men not climbed because of their devotion to their native land? Or who would do for love of money what the saints have done for love of God? Soul is not a synonym for softness nor spirit an equivalent of unreality. Men have suffered crucifixion rather than betray what they called their "conscience," and because of their devotion to "the will of God" other men have cheerfully faced the lions of the Roman arenas and the torture chambers of the Spanish Inquisition, the dungeons of Hitler and the concentration camps of Stalin, the loss of their jobs, the misunderstanding of their friends and their families, and the utter denial of their own personal hopes and ambitions.

Why have missionaries left behind the comfort of this well-favored land and gone to live and labor in all the far and fearful places of the earth? Certainly not for the fun of it. Surely not because they wanted to visit relatives, or hoped to make money, or sought to be famous. Why have mothers sacrificed themselves for their children, men laid down their lives for their friends, ill-paid teachers stayed on in their classrooms? Or think about Paul and the record of his life as he sets it down in the Second Letter to the Corinthians:

Five times I have received at the hands of the Jews the forty lashes less one. Three times I have been beaten with rods; once I was stoned. Three times I have been shipwrecked; a night and a day I have been adrift at sea; on frequent journeys, in danger from rivers, danger from robbers, danger from my own people, danger from Gentiles, danger in the city, danger in the wilderness, danger at sea, danger from false brethren; in toil and hardship, through many a sleepless night, in hunger and thirst, often without food, in cold and exposure. And, apart from other things, there is the daily pressure upon me of my anxiety for all the churches.

Remember that Paul's endurance of these sufferings was not compulsory but voluntary, and then try to call the invisible, inaudible, intangible motives which drove him to them nothing but illusions!

And when we think about any life which we can know beyond the one we know on earth, how can we escape the fact that if anything remains, it cannot be the material and must be the spiritual? "The Lord Christ *may* prove a vain hope," writes Dick Sheppard, "but one thing is clear: all the others who have defied Him and ignored Him have already been proved to be false prophets." And if there is no real assurance in a life of the spirit beyond the life of the body, to whom else or to what else shall we turn? If anything is certain in this life, it would appear to be the conclusion that the things which are seen are temporal; and if anything is eternal, it must fall within the sphere of the things which are unseen. We may think at first that we would rather have it otherwise, and we may feel that facing such a prospect, we have scant cause for confidence that we shall truly live beyond our body's death. But what other hope do we have? What other vehicle? What other way?

That is why Jesus counseled men not to lay up their treasures in earthly things: the treasures of earth are not transportable across the bridge to heaven. That is why he said that it would be difficult for a rich man to enter into God's kingdom: having all of his faith in the currency of things which are seen, he would find it hard to make the exchange into the currency of things which are not seen. That is why he told his followers to have no fear for those who could do no more than kill the body and to fear only that which could kill the soul: the material is good but not supremely good, and the earthly has significance but not everlasting significance.

In the year 1868 General Mariano Melgarejo, the dictator of Bolivia, invited the British minister to attend a reception in honor of his new mistress, and when the diplomat firmly declined, the affronted dictator had him tied to a donkey, facing aft, and trotted him three times around the main square of La Paz. The minister fled home and told Queen Victoria about the outrage. "Where is Bolivia?" the Queen demanded, and when a map had been brought to her, there is a perhaps apocryphal report that she took a pen, scratched a few lines across the paper, and haughtily declared: "Bolivia no longer exists!"

For one reason or another that is the way many people have felt about the realms of the spirit, but just as the pen scratches on the map did not eliminate Bolivia, so our lack of faith does not destroy the realms of the spirit. They are not deceptions, and they are not illusions. They actually exist. They are everlasting, and they are eternal. And facing both the profound mystery and the tremendous importance of the emphasis which Jesus put upon them, we could do worse than follow the example of a famous philosopher when someone had asked him: "Do you fully understand the Einstein theory of relativity? Do you go with him all the way?" "I answer the first question in the negative," the philosopher replied, "and the second in the affirmative."

Chapter II

FOLLOW ME

If any man would come after me, let him deny himself and take up his cross and follow me.   MATT. 16:24

SOMETIMES WE DO NOT FOLLOW JESUS BECAUSE WE DO NOT KNOW how, but at other times we do not follow him because we do not know why. It is not that we fail to understand what following Jesus means. It is only that seeing the road and finding it hard, we have not discovered any compelling reason for undertaking such an arduous and seemingly unrewarding journey.

Jesus indicated that before a man could follow him, he must "deny himself" and "take up his cross." Such words grate harshly on the modern ear, and it is scarcely strange that when we try to lodge the Christian faith in other people's hearts, we often meet resistance. "Why should I go through all that?" a man will ask us. "I'm getting along all right as I am. Why should I go to church on Sunday mornings? I like to play golf, or I like the extra sleep, or I've got a lot of work to do around the house and grounds. Why should I teach Sunday school? All the parents do is criticize, and all the children do is squirm. And why should I serve on church committees? They take me out evenings, and I want the time at home."

We sometimes wonder why the life of those who do not belong to the church often seems more attractive than that of church members, but why shouldn't it? People who do not belong to the church can spend more time in the beauty parlors: the every member canvass does not stop at their doors. They can have their lobster and their caviar: they do not have to give to missions. They have plenty of time at home: they are not singing in the choir or serving on the standing committee. They can be relaxed and well-adjusted: they do not have to think about anyone except themselves.

When someone outside the church takes a look at a life like that and asks why he should give it up to become a Christian, we had better have an answer ready. He has a strong case. He has a good argument. And in the dark days when we ask the same question ourselves, it will be good if we have given the matter sober thought in brighter times. The temptation to surrender is great. The allurements of defection are strong.

I

Of course, it has to be said at once that most of the people who ask that question are starting with the wrong assumption. The query which they really want to have answered might be phrased in words like these: "What am I going to get out of it myself? What is there in it for me?" And that is approaching the horse from the wrong end; for the reason for becoming a Christian is not a selfish one at all, and the purpose of following Christ is not to get but to give.

One day in El Paso, Texas, a man held up a motion picture theater and later told a radio audience that he became a robber "by being lucky and having faith," and many people falsely assume that Christianity's principal claim is to further our self-determined ends. If we want peace of mind, Christianity will give it to us. If we want to be successful in business, Christianity will bring us that success. If we are having trouble in marriage, Christianity will straighten us out. Questioning the authenticity of that claim, the skeptics throw out the true with the false, and when anybody approaches the Christian faith with these presuppositions, it is our duty to disabuse him at once of his misconceptions.

People who come to Christianity in search of peace of mind need to be reminded of Jesus' statement that he came not to bring peace but a sword. People who want to use Christianity as a highway to success must be pointed to the fallacy of James and John, who thought that being followers of Jesus meant sitting on his right and left in the kingdom of God and who had to be told that following Jesus meant bearing a cross. And people who think of Christianity as nothing but a way to solve the problem of their differences with others will have to read once more those words of Jesus when he said that he had come so to set a man at variance with those nearest to him that a man's foes would be those of his own household.

Mary Brent Whiteside has a poem called "Who Has Known Heights":

> Who has known heights and depths, shall not again
>   Know peace—not as the calm heart knows
>   Low, ivied walls; a garden close;
>   The old enchantment of a rose.
> And though he tread the humble ways of men,
> He shall not speak the common tongue again.
>
> Who has known heights, shall bear forevermore
>   An incommunicable thing
>   That hurts his heart, as if a wing
>   Beat at the portal, challenging;
> And yet—lured by the gleam his vision wore—
> Who once has trodden stars seeks peace no more.[1]

That insight is basic to an understanding of the reasons for becoming a Christian. We do not follow Jesus for the sake of personal comfort or advantage, and if the Christian faith has never repelled and even frightened us, we have never understood it.

II

The real foundation for the decision to become a Christian is the conviction that the Christian faith is true—absolutely true,

[1] Used by permission.

objectively true, finally true. Whether we like them or not, the Christian beliefs about God are accurate descriptions of God's nature and activity. Whether we like them or not, Christ's life and teaching represent God's will for every man who ever lives upon the earth. Whether we like it or not, the church is a part of God's plan for the establishment of his kingdom among men, and, in the deepest sense of the words, it is literally true that he who does not have the church for his mother cannot have God as his Father.

It was not a Christian minister but the famous psychiatrist James Tucker Fisher who made this comment about the teachings of Jesus:

If you were to take the sum total of all the authoritative articles ever written by the most qualified of psychologists and psychiatrists . . . if you were to take the whole of the meat and none of the parsley, and if you were to have these unadulterated bits of pure scientific knowledge concisely expressed by the most capable of living poets, you would have an awkward and incomplete summation of the Sermon on the Mount.[2]

So it is throughout the length and breadth of human experience. Whatever the point at which it touches man's life on the earth, the Christian faith is not indulging in wishful fancies: it is speaking the sober and unavoidable truth, and they who live by other laws are like the man in Milwaukee who, being arrested for drunkenness and asked by the police why he was riding a streetcar early Tuesday morning without any pants, explained that he thought it was Monday. When we live as if the Christian faith were not true, we dwell in a dream world as dangerous as that of a man who lives as if the laws of gravity were not true; and sooner or later our airy castles will come crashing down upon our heads to prove again that God is not mocked and that whatsoever a man sows, that shall he also reap.

[2] *Time*, May 28, 1951.

III

The second reason for becoming a Christian will seem at first to contradict the caution against following Jesus for the sake of personal advantage, but how can we escape the obvious meaning of Jesus' words when he says that the seeming losses of the Christian are really gains and the apparent liabilities actually assets? Those who sacrificed themselves for his sake need not worry, he said: their lost lives would be restored to them washed clean of weakness and stain. Those who had forsaken houses and lands or loved ones and friends in his name need have no concern: they would "receive a hundredfold" and "inherit eternal life." The pure in heart would see God. The peacemakers would be called God's children. The persecuted would inherit God's kingdom.

It is one of the compelling elements in Jesus' teaching that while he did not use rewards as bribes to gain adherents, he often reassured his followers that the fruits of the spirit were noncompetitive possessions and that the more they gave to other people, the more they would have for themselves; and it is one of the incidental but steadying reasons for being a Christian that contemporary experience confirms the teaching of Jesus.

Here, for example, is the testimony of John S. Bonnell concerning patients who go to the operating table with a confident faith in God. They

take less anaesthetic, recover from it more easily and with far less of the usual distressing after-effects. They have little or no restlessness. . . . They have a quicker and less eventful convalescence. They carry out the doctor's orders better.[3]

Here are the words of Lawrence Zellers, one of the small group of Methodist missionaries who were held captive for about three years by the North Korean forces:

[3] *Pastoral Psychology*, Sept., 1953.

23

In our association with the prisoners of war, one could easily see the difference between those men who had spiritual fiber and those who lacked it. The latter died in by far the larger numbers. . . . After living among these prisoners of war for a year, I felt, as did most of the other missionaries, that the lack of a religious faith was responsible for more deaths than any other cause except the starvation diet.[4]

And in the wider realm of social policy here are our vain attempts to avoid the obvious demands of Christian conscience by maintaining "separate but equal" facilities for white people and black people in some parts of the country and our slow discovery that such a segregated procedure is not only unchristian but moreover so staggering in cost that few communities can pay for it.

Some time ago *Life* magazine printed a full-page picture entitled "Canned Pig." "The object beautifully framed on this silvery milk can, held up against the white and azure sky like a rare gem set in platinum," the caption read, "is . . . a pig. The pig entered the can on June 12 to lap up some milk, got so bloated that it was unable to back out." The owner saved both pig and can by doing nothing. After eight hours of enforced dieting, the animal shrank down to size and got out by itself.

They who have ears to hear do well to hearken to the parable of the pig. The self-seeking life is the self-defeating life, and though the fasting and prayer of Christian discipline are aimed at the service of others, they also represent the only avenue to spiritual freedom and continuing growth. When we seek the Christian faith for selfish ends, we are first frustrated and ultimately destroyed; but when we follow Jesus for his sake and God's, we find our crosses turned to wings.

IV

And so with all concerns of truth and self behind us, we come at last to the trigger of Christian decision. We might describe it

[4] *The Christian Century,* June 17, 1953.

simply in the words the French employ in saying, *"Noblesse oblige."* Or we might speak instead as Jesus did: "Every one to whom much is given, of him will much be required."

Rank imposes obligation. Privilege involves responsibility. Ownership is stewardship. Freely we have received, and freely must we therefore give.

The man who sits back in his easy chair and blandly asks why he should become a Christian is usually blind to one of the most terrible facts of our day—the fact that Christians are at war, that this war is a life and death struggle, and that for good or for bad the issue of the conflict will have immeasurable consequences for himself, for those he loves, and for all men everywhere. The most obvious incarnation of the warfare now is the contest between the Christian interpretation of human life and the Communist interpretation. There cannot be the slightest doubt that the Communists are furthering their ends by all the means in their control, and any man who says that there is no reason for him to become a Christian because he is all right as he is had better understand as quickly as possible that unless he stirs himself from his lethargy, he will not be all right very long. But this is not the only battle which Christians are waging today. We are waging a battle against poverty, against homelessness, against injustice, against the religious ignorance of our children, against banality and sensuality and the cult of despair. These are not military games. These are not mock battles. These are fights to the death, and the man who takes them lightly would do well to realize at once that the time is shorter than he thinks.

It is not hard for anyone to understand the mood of Henry Watson Fowler when at the age of forty-one he retired from his position as a schoolmaster with the solemn announcement, "I'm never going to do a useful thing again." Sooner or later everybody gets tired of duty, weary of responsibility, fed up with being helpful; but to eat the fruits of Christian faith and never plant the trees is both to be a parasite upon the past and to steal our own comfort from the pain of our fellows.

"Why should I be a Christian? I'm all right as I am." A strange question that, for asking it we are the man who stands on the river bank and seeing a woman drowning asks why he should get himself wet by going to her rescue: he is all right as he is. Or we are the man who happens on a house afire, where everyone is desperately trying to save trapped children, carry out movable furniture, extinguish the flames; and we ask why we should get all dirty by lending our help: we are all right as we are. Or we are the man who sits on the cellar stairs smoking his pipe while his wife struggles up toward the kitchen with the heavy laundry basket. Why should he get up to help her? He is all right as he is. Of course, in such circumstances we have our reward: we are dry and clean and comfortable. But our prize is a terrible prize, and we stand beneath the condemnation of the words of James: "Whoever knows what is right to do and fails to do it, for him it is sin."

Who do I think I am, that I *deserve* the shelter of my warm, oil-heated house while that ill-clad family in Korea huddles in its windy, wooden shack and its youngest daughter dies of pneumonia? Who do I think I am, that I *deserve* to eat my steaks and chops while coughing refugees in Europe eat potato soup and perish of tuberculosis? Who do I think I am, that I *deserve* the riches of this land of the free and home of the brave which my fathers died to achieve and my brothers died to preserve?

The contented pagan says that he does not need the Christian faith: he is comfortable already. But his comfort is his condemnation. He says that he does not have to be a Christian: he is happy just as he is. But his happiness is the sign of his sin. He calls himself a man who can love both God and his neighbor without being a Christian, but God replies that they who love him feed his sheep.

For those who daily reap the fruits of Christian faithfulness the making of a compensating contribution is a matter of simple decency. Any worthy man wants to pull his own weight in the boat. Any worthy man wants to carry his own share of the burden. And when the struggle is as crucial as the one we face today and when every man worth his salt is exerting his utmost effort to push the Christian cause to victory, then malingerers must stand the awful scrutiny of words like those King Henry sent to Crillon: "Hang yourself, brave Crillon: we have fought at Arques and you were not there."

"Why should I become a Christian? I'm all right as I am."

That man is not all right: he is completely and utterly wrong! He is living on dwindling capital. He is fiddling while Rome burns. He is sitting on a powder keg whose fuse has been lighted. He is draining the blood of the men who bear his burdens for him. It is inescapably hard to follow Jesus, but sooner or later we shall find that in a world like our own it is even harder not to follow him.

Chapter III

LOVE YOUR NEIGHBOR

You shall love your neighbor." MATT. 22:39

THE LOVE OF OUR NEIGHBOR HAS ITS ORIGIN IN THOSE WORDS OF John which seem at first remote from it. "God so loved the world," he wrote, "that he gave his only Son, that whoever believes in him should not perish but have eternal life."

Many have said that this is the whole of Christianity, expressed in its briefest possible form, and few would quarrel with the claim that these words constitute one of the central affirmations of the Christian gospel. But indifference grows quickly out of familiarity, and for the understanding of the nature of God's love the whole becomes more meaningful if we first consider one of its parts: "God so loved . . . that he gave . . ."

I

"God so loved that he gave." John names Jesus as the special gift which God made to the world because of his love, and in the carpenter of Nazareth there was uniqueness which will always lift him high above all other gifts which God has ever given man. Paul saw clearly when he said that "God was in Christ," and nowhere on the earth has God chosen to reveal himself again with such completeness and finality as he displayed in this strange man who walked beside the Galilean lake almost two thousand years ago.

Yet it is a part of our faith in Jesus himself that there is more to God than his Son, and it is one of our reasons for believing that Jesus was really divine that through the confinements and the limitations of a single, earthly, human life he showed us so definitively what God is like—everywhere and always. Jesus the man was but an audible and visible symbol of God's constant character, decisions, and acts. It was not simply that God so loved the world nineteen hundred years ago that he gave his only Son to the people who happened to live in Palestine at that time. God *always* so loves that he gives. He gives his Son, but he gives much more than his Son; and we have not even begun to understand God's nature and will until we see him daily so loving people that he pours out himself for their welfare.

"You were bought with a price," Paul told the Corinthians and how great a price God paid and still pays for the life and growth of his creatures we seldom stop to think or ask. To begin the cultivation of that awareness, we need only consider the words of Sir James Baillie when he says, "It is very significant that the whole firmament of heaven has to be set ablaze to bring out the full glory of the dewdrop on the daisy." Or we may think of Roland H. Bainton pointing out that our expression "vocational guidance" comes directly from Martin Luther. God has called men to labor, Luther saw, because he himself labors.

God is a tailor who makes for the deer a coat that will last for a thousand years. He is a shoemaker also who provides boots that the deer will not outlive. God is the best cook, because the heat of the sun supplies all the heat there is for cooking. God is a butler who sets forth a feast for the sparrows and spends on them annually more than the total revenue of the king of France.[1]

Or we may remember such common tasks as growing vegetables or painting houses. A man is a farmer, let us say, and no one needs to tell him how much toil he spends to make his crops grow—how much plowing, harrowing, planting, weeding, watering, fertilizing, spraying. But do we also recall how much time and effort God has to spend too—how much creating, warming, watering, feeding,

[1] *Here I Stand* (New York and Nashville: Abingdon Press, 1950), p. 233.

enlivening? Or perhaps a man paints his house, and when the mixing and the application of the paint have been finished, he says that the job is done. But that is not true; for the paint is still wet, and while he goes in to wash his hands and sit down for his evening meal, God takes over and dries his house for him. And it is no escape to call the universe a great machine which God created in the beginning, set running, and then left to do its job alone; for whoever heard of a machine which needs no tending?

In her collection of poems entitled *Saints Without Tears,* Phyllis McGinley has a poem called "The Temptation of St. Anthony":

> Off in the wilderness bare and level,
> Anthony wrestled with the Devil.
> Once he'd beaten the Devil down,
> Anthony'd turn his eyes toward town
> And leave his hermitage now and then
> To come to grips with the souls of men.
>
> Afterwards, all the tales agree,
> Wrestling the Devil seemed to be
> Quite a relief to Anthony.[2]

Are we to suppose that God never feels like that about the stubborn people he has made? Are we to assume that God never wonders whether he was wrong in creating human beings in the first place? Are we to be sure that God never longs for the peace of some "wilderness" bare of all the problems men have caused him?

But God so loves that he gives. He gives the sunlight and the shadow, the mountains and the meadows, food and water, loved ones and friends, work and play, life and death, and life that conquers death. For when we speak about the love of God, we speak about a kind of love whose nature is not to seek and grasp and hold, but to give.

[2] From *The Love Letters of Phyllis McGinley.* Used by permission of Viking Press.

II

And for nineteen hundred years, putting their trust in this loving God as Jesus Christ revealed him, men have found that the love of God cannot be separated from the love of man. Because God first loved them, they have found the will and the power to love their neighbors, and thus a bridge has been built between God and man, between heaven and earth, between eternity and time. Not all of the men of these years have loved in this manner. Not even all of the Christians of these years have so loved. But when we call to mind the greatest benefactors of the world in these long centuries since Christ was born, we find that they have loved their neighbors as God himself first loved them and that because they have loved, they have given.

First of all, there were the followers of Jesus during his life on the earth, the few dozen men who were closest to him in his ministry and who bore the largest burden of responsibility for his gospel after his death. Surely they so loved that they gave—gave not merely their idle hours and their superfluous possessions, gave not simply one-tenth of their income or one-half of their income, but gave their peace of mind, their community positions, their family ties, their means of livelihood, their lives.

Then there were the martyrs of the centuries which followed; and thinking about them, we see in our minds the Roman arenas, the lions, the gladiatorial combats, the blazing torches of Nero. We remember the racks and the stakes of the Spanish Inquisition and the Protestant Reformation. We watch the saintly core of Pilgrims braving wintry seas on the Mayflower and other vessels bent on similar mission. How great must have been the love of men and women like these that they should give so freely of themselves in support of that love—love of God, love of Christ, love of righteousness!

A few days after the birth of Isaac Watts his father began a term of more than a year in the jail at Southampton because he believed he had the right to worship in the fellowship led by the Rev. Nathaniel Robinson rather than in the established church and that other people also had that right. Every day his wife took the infant Isaac to the jail, and seated on the horseblock outside the entrance, she fed the child in the sight of his imprisoned father. When Isaac was nine years old, the elder Watts began another six months of imprisonment for the same reason and after his release spent two years away from his family, in hiding in London. And was it not love which drove him to such a giving of himself—love of freedom, love of truth, love of his fellow men?

In the early days of the missionary effort in this country the hardships were so great that there were more missionaries who died than there were converts who were baptized. One of the missionaries at that time was Lucian Farnham, a student at Andover Theological Seminary who chose the home field as the site of his labors, and this is what he had to say about his work in Illinois:

Late in the autumn of that year I arrived in this state where I have labored to this time, in season and out of season—in ceiled houses and log cabins, in school houses, in private dwellings, and in the open air without a house. I have traveled many thousands of miles through heat and cold, storm and calm, by night and day, in perils in the wilderness, in perils in the prairie, in perils of waters—in hunger and thirst, in weariness and painfulness, in watchings and fastings—I have made my lodging in the lone prairie without food or fire—with no shelter but heaven's canopy—no bed but the open wagon-box, and no music but the howling of the wolf . . . . By the grace of God I am what I am. It is wonderful condescension that God should give me a place in His vineyard.

And was it not love which drove Farnham to such a giving of himself—love of Jesus, love of God, love of the people whom he was trying to reach with the gospel?

Florence Nightingale, Father Damien, Albert Schweitzer, Frank

Laubach; Christian doctors, nurses, statesmen, teachers, fathers and mothers—let the roots of their lives be uncovered, and always we find a love which is so great that it has no choice but to give; and if the reasons for that love were reduced to purely rational terms, they would probably be expressed in the firm conviction that the only force which can be counted upon to prevail in the world is the unmeasured expenditure of self which is girded and guided by Christian love.

If the experience of the Christian centuries has taught us nothing else, it has certainly shown us that there is no salvation for the world short of vast inequalities in the burdens which some men will be called upon to carry, short of fearful disparities in pleasure and profit, short of tremendous sacrifice on the part of some for the sake of others. In I Kings we find these revealing words about Adonijah, one of the sons of David and Haggith: "Now Adonijah the son of Haggith exalted himself, saying, 'I will be king': *and he prepared for himself chariots and horsemen, and fifty men to run before him."* [3] These have been the commonly accepted evidences of kingship in every age and generation—thrones and scepters, power and prestige, pomp and circumstance. But the Christian saints have always known that there is a far better standard of kingship and that this is the love of the neighbor, the sacrificial love with which God himself first loved us.

III

So we come at last to ourselves, and it becomes apparent that the deep things of the spirit recognize no boundaries of time or person or place. They invade our own hearts. They ask us questions. They demand obedience.

For many weeks I was once engaged in correspondence with a man whom I have never met and who first wrote to me in disagreement with something which I had said in a radio broadcast. His

[3] Italics mine.

letters were steadily critical of the church, and at first I thought that he was "just a fanatic." But as letter after letter came from him, I found a soundness in them which I could not laugh away, and here is part of one of them:

It was not my intent to suggest the elimination of the church as a group. To the extent that the church encourages and stimulates the reading of the Scripture, it has probably helped people to do more than they might otherwise do; for I know no other book which teaches that we should love and do good to our neighbors, enemies, and in fact every one. But somewhere along the line something is woefully lacking when thousands and even millions of children are dying of things we could prevent or cure while we build fine homes, buy fine cars, and erect fine churches. We think it terrible when a drinking man uses his money for liquor instead of needed food for his family, but if he is wealthy enough to drink and still feed his family, there is little protest. I am protesting against *any* expense, except to extend life, as long as lives are being lost which could be saved or extended through the effort being spent in other ways. . . . It is my belief that a person who deliberately refuses (as I am doing and I presume you are doing) to help save these lives is but a step—and a very little one!—higher than the person who deliberately shortens a life. Maybe we are even worse in God's sight because added knowledge has given to us added responsibility. . . . A family which had a sick or starving child and did not themselves give up everything but the barest essentials to save its life would be a poor family in my sight. It might be tough to see the other children working when we would like to see them playing or in school. If the struggle continued year after year, it would become most heartbreaking. We would hardly blame them if some of the children finally gave up the battle, deserted their family, and went out to make their own way in the world. But would any success they ever attained be worth the life of that brother or sister if they should die because of that decision? . . . Regardless of your clothes, your sermons, or anything else, I know that you have deserted your brother and left him to die while you sought success for yourself. You know the same in regard to me and others. We know that in a pinch we can't be depended on. On the battlefield we would leave the wounded to die. At the seashore we would not be interested in preventing drowning: we would solicit money for churches instead of a lifeguard. If one of our houses were burning, we would look up our insurance policies instead of saving the lives of the people who were trapped in the house.

These letters from my unmet correspondent still trouble me. He does not see all of the picture any more than I see all of it myself, but he sees a part of it which is never seen at all by many people in the churches, and he makes the loving of our neighbors uncomfortably contemporary. When Peter said that he loved Jesus, he was given the simple commandment which would henceforth serve as the test of that love: "Feed my lambs." The lambs, of course, were people; and they still are—our friends and our relatives, our fellow townsmen and our fellow Americans, but also the overburdened agricultural workers of northern Greece, the refugees made homeless by fire in Korea, the starving millions of India, the rebels fleeing from East Germany and Hungary. When Jesus commanded that Peter should "feed" his lambs, he meant, of course, that Peter should make provision for all of the needs of God's people; and he still does—the hunger of the stomach, but also the hunger of the heart and the mind and the soul, the ache of loneliness, the gnaw of guilt, the chains of self, the icy grip of fear. Whatever faults the letters of my disturbing correspondent may have, at least they see clearly the profound truth which John had sighted as he thought about the relationship between God and Jesus. When someone loves, he gives; and the measure of his giving is also the measure of his loving.

My correspondent has lost most of his faith in the church, but I do not share his lack of confidence. The church is still the body of Christ in the world today—his lips to speak his gospel, his feet to run his errands, his hands to work his healing ministry upon the troubled ways of men. The church is still the holy fellowship of those who love both God and other men as God himself has first loved them. The church is still God's chosen means to feed his lambs.

The commandment to Peter is the commandment to every Christian man or woman: When we love, we feed. The discovery of the saints belongs to all of us: there is no road to victory except the road of sacrifice. But one bright day we make that further discovery, which God himself made at the end of his labors in creation: we look upon our deeds of self-denial, and we find that they have been good. We see that in those hours when we have truly served the Lord, we have done so with gladness. We learn what Jesus meant when he said that it is more blessed to give than to receive—that is, more satisfying, more happy, more joyous, more Godlike. And then thanksgiving becomes for us not simply an annual observance but rather a daily experience; for we have known in our own hearts the truth that every authentic cross has a resurrection and every true Calvary an Easter dawn. Because God loves us, we love our neighbor; and loving our neighbor, we praise our Father.

Chapter IV

DO NOT GIVE DOGS WHAT IS HOLY

Do not give dogs what is holy; and do not throw your pearls before swine, lest they trample them underfoot and turn to attack you. MATT. 7:6

THESE WORDS DO NOT SOUND LIKE JESUS' WORDS. THEY ARE TOO abrupt. They are too harsh. Their garments look like those of bitterness and cruelty, and their voice has little obvious relationship to this man whom the centuries have always described in terms of tenderness and love.

Yet it is hard to believe that these words constitute an exception to Jesus' normal courtesy and thoughtfulness. In the fury of his anger there were days when he could call the scribes and Pharisees "hypocrites" and "blind guides" and when he could even compare them to whitewashed tombs full of dead men's bones, but it was not his way to call people "dogs" nor to speak of human beings as "swine." He who loved little children, who sent out his disciples to heal the sick and cleanse the lepers, who spent so much of his time among the disinherited poor, whose counsel was to give drink to the thirsty and clothes to the naked and companionship to those confined in prison—he was not a man to be unkind or rude or uncouth, and whatever else we may think about this strange admonition to his followers, it is reasonable to suppose at the outset that it was nothing which could not be said by a cultured and sensitive man who held in the highest respect the selfhood of every creature God had made in human form.

Somewhere near the center of his meaning there must have been a warning such as this: "Don't be absurd in what you try to do in my name." It was not because pigs were despicable creatures that a man refrained from casting his pearls to them: it was only that in the providence of God's kingdom pigs had no awareness of the use or importance of pearls. And it was not because dogs were evil that one kept his holy things away from them: it was simply that God had so made dogs that they would derive no more benefit from holy things than from a carpenter's hammer or a fisherman's knife.

When Jesus spoke about the folly of giving holy things to dogs and throwing pearls to swine, it was like saying that a man ought not to plant his seeds in the middle of a concrete highway, or carry his water in a bucket with a hole in its bottom, or saw his boards with a screw driver, or use ten-dollar bills to roll cigarettes. Men were not to leave their brains at home on the day when they volunteered for service in his band of disciples. They were to have the harmlessness of doves, but they were also to have the wisdom of serpents. He expected them to maintain a fine sense of the fitness of things. He expected them to cultivate a proper respect for the priceless; and if they bought the world, he did not want the currency to be their souls.

Specifically, it was the folly of waste which Jesus was describing in these words. Waste of time. Waste of energy. Waste of resources. Every man on earth has treasure in his hands, he was saying. Every man on earth is a sexton of things precious, a custodian of things holy; and it is nothing less than sin that anyone treat scornfully what God himself has given and no man ever could replace.

I

The warning is no less needed now than nineteen hundred years ago, and think first about individuals—the one man or the one woman whom God has made each of us and for whom we have primary and inescapable responsibility. If we are searching for treasure, we need go no farther. If we are looking for something holy, we can stop right here.

Some people think too highly of themselves, but others think too little. If we were created in the image of God, if we were made but little lower than the angels and crowned with glory and honor, if we are the children of God's love and care and are held in such high esteem by him that he gave his only begotten Son for our salvation —the least of us is great in God's sight, and we do no more than scorn the one who made us if we despise the people he has made. In the eyes of God each person on earth is a pearl of great price. Everyone is holy. But still we throw our pearls before swine and give our holy things to dogs.

Here, for example, is a poll of young people which Lawrence A. Averill conducted a few years ago with reference to their heroes and heroines. Gene Autry defeated Jesus Christ by four to one; Jack Benny was given as many votes as all the ministers, priests, and missionaries combined; and twice as many girls wanted to be like Shirley Temple or Jane Powell as longed to resemble all of the religious figures in the world's history. As this book is being prepared for the printer, the names have changed; and before it reaches the reader, they will have changed again. But will anyone claim that the substitution of Elvis Presley for Gene Autry has substantially improved the situation?

Or here is *Time's* review of Tchaikovsky's *Nutcracker Suite* in the recording of Spike Jones and his City Slickers: "The *Sugar Plum Fairy* danced to a set of camel bells, the *Arabs* to an accompaniment of carefully modulated burps. Tchaikovsky's flutes, piccolos and muted strings were drowned out by washboards, police sirens, breaking glass." [1]

Or still further, here is a newspaper report about a Boston boy who was arrested for shooting a druggist with a pistol he had stolen from a state police barracks. His father told the police that his son's downfall had been caused by reading comic books. He

[1] December 17, 1945.

said that he had torn up about ten dollars' worth of the books in a year, but it did no good because his son would always buy more.

To what are we really devoting these lives of ours? For what are we selling our souls? What are the ends toward which we are striving? Far too often the answer is something like this: "I want the social standing which comes from owning a house in the best part of town and holding membership in the best clubs and societies. I want a television set in my living room and a freezer in my basement. I want to be known as a man who makes $25,000 a year and has a summer home in Maine and a winter vacation in Florida. I want to be popular. I want to be admired. I want to be envied. For my old age I want security, and for my present life I want comfort, pleasure, prestige, and power."

But on these goals which we have set for ourselves the words of Jesus speak a steady condemnation. "It is your souls which you are selling," he warns us. "It is your lives which you are wasting. It is not that all of your pleasures are wicked or all of your gadgets evil: it is only that human life was never meant to become preoccupied with these matters. It is not that man's approval is wrong or that the powers of earth are sinful: it is only that they were never intended to be man's gods and that they have no enduring relationship to man's most important concerns. For a man's life does not consist in the abundance of the things which he possesses—not even in expensive automobiles or fine houses. Life is more than meat—more even than charcoal broiled steaks and lobster thermidor. The body is more than raiment—more even than a Parisian dress or a Park Avenue hat. Man does not live by bread alone—nor even by titled positions or recognition in the newspapers. For what shall it profit a man if he gains the whole world but loses his own soul?"

Jesus would doubtless have enjoyed Frank Tashlin's story called *The Bear That Wasn't*. One cold autumn day the bear realizes that winter is near, and obeying the instincts which God has given him, he waddles into hibernation. While he sleeps, workmen arrive and build a big factory over his cave. By spring the factory is finished, and when the bear trundles out, he finds that his forest is wholly changed. The factory foreman thinks that he is just a worker in a fur coat, and he orders him back to his job. When the bear protests that he is really a bear, he is sent through channels all the way up to the president of the company. The other officials insist that he is just a silly man in a fur coat who needs a shave, but the president decides that the matter needs further investigation. So they take him to the zoo and ask the other bears what they think. For a time the bears are a little puzzled, but they finally conclude that the bear cannot be a bear because he is on the wrong side of the bars. Then they take him to the circus where the trained bears are riding around a ring on bicycles, with balloons in their paws and trick hats on their heads, but the circus bears give the same verdict: the bear is not a bear because he does not have a hat, a balloon, and a bicycle. Finally the bear himself is convinced that he has been wrong. He is really only a silly man in a fur coat who needs a shave. So he goes to work in the factory, and all the officials congratulate one another on solving a difficult problem.

But months later the factory closes, and the bear is paid off like the workers. Still convinced that he is a man, he wanders back to his own kind of civilization. When autumn comes, he starts automatically for his cave, but suddenly he remembers that he is not a bear and therefore cannot hibernate. With the advent of winter he almost freezes to death. He knows what bears do in the winter but not what men do, and he spends his days in wretchedness and misery. But as he sits there trembling in the cold, he finally makes up his mind that he was right in the beginning. He is not a man at all: he is a bear! So he goes back to his cave, and folding his paws, he sinks into blissful hibernation.[2]

It is an insight such as this which Jesus demanded. "It is a matter of the utmost consequence that you make up your minds

[2] Used by permission.

who you really are," he was saying to those who would listen to him. "You are not just animals. You are not even simply human beings. You are God's children, and the ways of life appropriate to any other level of existence are not intended for you."

Among the children of God it is the real goal of life that they know their Father, that they love him, and that they share with him the blessed work of building, healing, and helping. It is in this goal alone that the spending of the self involves the saving of the self, and any other purpose man assigns to his earthly life will always prove a fruitless purpose. It will mean dumping lives on garbage heaps and pouring souls down sink drains. It will mean giving holy things to dogs and throwing pearls before swine.

II

So much for individuals. Think now about the larger social structure in which each of us is a part.

Consider, for example, the inexcusable waste of our natural resources. Year after year in the coastal towns where herring are seined, the Department of Sea and Shore Fisheries in one of our New England states fought a steady battle with companies which had no use for the fish themselves and wanted only their scales for the manufacture of costume jewelry. So they put the fish through scaling devices and then dumped them back into the ocean to die and by their dead bodies on the bottom of a cove or inlet ruin a weir or seining place for many years to come. Early hunters in the woods shooting down the moose, in part for the sport and in part for the hides, but then leaving the uncounted pounds of edible flesh to rot away unused; lumberjacks not bothering to put out their fires because once the white pine was cut away, the rest of the woods had no value; farmers refusing to rotate their crops or to use the contour plowing which would prevent the erosion of the soil from their lands; food grown and then destroyed to keep prices up; food grown and then stored away underground while overseas the people starved for want of it—what a record man has made of squandering the bounty of the earth and putting it to uses which God never intended and does not approve!

Or think about the equally inexcusable waste of our human resources. One of the most interesting social facts about newspapers, writes Robert Lasch,

is the altogether disproportionate and often ridiculous mobilization of great technical resources for trivial ends. The news-plane speeds to the scene, the reporters flash their findings to a waiting desk, photographers slap excellent pictures on the wire-photo network, engravers and ty-pographers translate words and pictures into metal, bells ring, presses roll —and the newspaper hits the street with screaming headlines about a cheap hussy slain in a love nest.

The prettiest girls in the nation go to Hollywood, the best actors, the most expert fashion designers, the ablest photographers, script-writers, beauticians, press agents, and directors. Time is spent without hesitation, and money is poured out with no restraint, and all the wisdom of the whole community is devoted to the production of many a motion picture which no intelligent adult will ever view without disgust or boredom. In the programs of radio and television the principal objection is not that the violence leads to murder nor that the sexual display incites to lust. It is only that what is offered is often not worth the time and money spent in its preparation and presentation, that precious resources are being wasted, and that a potent medium of communication is being prostituted to an end for which God never meant it.

Worst of all, think about the major social problem of our time: war. War always means the curtailment of any expense not essential to defense. It always means dragging to a halt anything constructive, anything which contributes to better understanding between the nations in conflict, anything which labors rather toward disinterested justice than toward victory in arms. Destruction is the order of the day, and toward that end war always takes the healthiest bodies and kills them. It takes the keenest minds and perverts them. It takes the finest woolen goods and cuts them into garments which can be used for nothing but uniforms. It takes the best rubber and turns it into tires which will fit nothing but military vehicles. It takes the strongest steel and builds it into tanks which have no place except on a battlefield.

The war in Korea will serve as a single, concrete example. In the three years between 1950 and 1953 this conflict involved the services of 5,000,000 men and cost the United States $22,000,000,000. In combat 1,430,000 soldiers were killed, and 250,000 more were wounded. In the struggle 400,000 Korean civilians died. One fourth of all Koreans were left homeless, and 100,000 children were made orphans. In North Korea 40 per cent of all habitations were destroyed, and the population was reduced from 8,000,000 to 4,000,000; and in South Korea 75 per cent of the mines and textile factories were put out of action, and two thirds of the schools were made unusable.

All this we know in our minds, but so many people never really know it in their hearts. For most of us in the United States of America war slips so easily into the category of things far away. We do not see the hurt and harm of it. We do not feel the pain and wrong of it. We do not understand the sin of it. High taxes are offensive to us, but the reason for our grimness with regard to them is more that we should have to part with the money than that the money is being used for wasteful and evil purposes. A chosen people singularly blessed with the good things of body and soul, we often find ourselves in the position of men whose very bounty has made them blind. For we are like a boy engaged in target practice with his rifle. At first he uses tin cans, bits of wood, and circles drawn on paper; but after a while that becomes uninteresting to him. So he goes into the house and spends a blissful afternoon shooting up the family treasures—a Staffordshire figurine, a Sandwich glass pitcher, a full-length mirror, a fine old watch.

Somewhere we seem to have conceived the idea that creation is easy for God. In the beginning God created the heaven and the earth, we read, and we imagine that the process must have been like a snapping of the fingers. But it was not so! Creation never comes easy, and the universe is no exception. The ancient legend that God created the world in six days preserves at least the fact that creation came hard for God. It took him time. He had to work at it. The mountains and the valleys, the oceans and the rivers, the trees and the grass and the flowers, the bodies of men and women, the brain, the mind, and the soul—there are sweat and tears in them. They were bought with a price, and the attitude that although regrettable war is yet easily justifiable fails to reckon with the utter dreadfulness of destroying God's property, the complete horror of tearing out of God's hands the control of man's living and dying.

"Do not give dogs what is holy," Jesus said, "and do not throw your pearls before swine." Do not indeed! The earth is the Lord's; it is not ours. We are his people: we do not belong to ourselves. We are but stewards of the holy things in our possession. We are only custodians of the pearls which we enjoy. And the owner of them does not want a fine clock to be used as a dishpan nor a piano employed as a boat.

Chapter V

LOVE YOUR ENEMIES

You have heard that it was said, "You shall love your neighbor and hate your enemy." But I say to you, Love your enemies and pray for those who persecute you, so that you may be sons of your Father who is in heaven.   MATT. 5:43-45

A FEW YEARS AGO I FOUND IN MY MAIL A LETTER FROM A TROUBLED man. He had been reading Matthew, and this was what he wrote to his pastor:

For a long time some of the verses in Matthew 5, which are said to be Matthew's report of the teachings of Jesus, have been a puzzle to me. Unless they *mean* something different than they *say*, I certainly cannot agree with them.

Elsewhere in the Bible we are taught to resist evil. Christ is said to have taken a whip to drive the tradesmen out of the temple. He resisted Satan in the wilderness. And today we believe that unless it is resisted, Communism will destroy Christianity.

If someone forced me to go with him while he committed a murder, I'd agree to go and do him one better if I followed the teachings of those verses. If someone entered my house to steal my piano, I'm taught to give him the rest of my furniture, if those verses are right. If someone espouses a cause which is commonly known to be wrong, unfair, and downright destructive, and it happens to affect my interests, I am to agree with him quickly, go along with *his* ideas, and go him one better if these verses are true.

I guess I've said enough to let you know why I'm puzzled. I'm inclined to doubt that Jesus ever said any such thing.

46

Of all the teachings of Jesus his command that we love our enemies is certainly one of the hardest to believe, approve, or obey, and this letter finds quick sympathy in almost anybody's heart. Turning the other cheek, going the second mile, not resisting one who is evil, making friends with your accuser, praying for the man who wrongs you—a life like that seems like a life of jumping off high buildings or feeding children broken glass or asking your cat to do the dishes; and not wanting to believe, we try to escape the necessity. Perhaps Matthew made a mistake in his record, we tell ourselves. Perhaps Jesus did not mean his words to be taken seriously. Or perhaps they were intended only for his own land and time, and nineteen hundred years have made a world so different that living now, Jesus would disown these words of long ago.

Yet inwardly we know that this commandment lies close to the heart of Jesus' whole gospel, that such a man would never speak such words without meaning them, and that this concept handles depths of life which time can never change. We can believe Jesus' words, or we can call them foolish. We can applaud them or scorn them. We can obey them or flaunt them. But however persistently we may wriggle, we can never quite escape the fact that this is what Jesus actually said, that he meant his words to be taken in utter seriousness, and that anyone who calls himself a Christian is under obligation to comply with them.

What then did Jesus have in mind when he said to his followers, "Love your enemies"? What are the implications of those words today? What do they mean for you and me?

I

For one thing, Jesus was certainly not referring to an act which, performed with literal exactness, would win for man the approval of God. There is nothing legalistic about this commandment of Jesus. "God's absolute will cannot be compressed into a law for this world," writes Martin Dibelius. "It can be set forth only in 'signs.' Therefore the demand of Jesus in its deepest meaning does not run: So must thou *act*, but rather, So must thou *be!*" Indeed, if obedience to Jesus' bidding in this matter were to be confined to the illustrations which he uses, many people would spend most of their lives without any opportunity to respond. It is not often that anyone smites us on the cheek, or sues us for our coat, or compels us to walk a mile with him; and although Jesus doubtless intended his followers to obey him precisely in each of these instances whenever the occasion arose, these examples were meant principally to be windows on the wide and sunny room of being with which he was really concerned. For it must have been as obvious to him as to us that the act of turning the other cheek or walking the second mile need not be synonymous with the kind of love which he was describing and that a man might obey the specific injunction without knowing the quality of heart and soul which gave the injunction its meaning and power.

Nor did Jesus mean that we are to love *just* our enemies or that we are to love our enemies more than our friends. Any decent man would love his friends, and Jesus was taking it for granted that he did not have to tell his disciples to do what they were already doing. In his commandment to love the enemy he was simply choosing an extreme case, the most extreme case of which he could think. His followers were to put no limits on their love, he was saying. They were to love everybody—their friends, their acquaintances, and even their enemies.

Still further, Jesus did not mean that we must like the enemies whom he commands us to love. When a boy and a girl decide to be married, they have liked each other before they have loved each other; but in the treatment of our enemies it is usually necessary that we love them before we like them, and every man will have many occasions to love people whom he will never like. The incredible diversity of human beings seems to indicate a providence of God in which each of us will like some people better than others and never like certain people at all. For the most part enemies are people whom we do not like, and although learning to love them may lead us also to like them, the fact that we dislike them has nothing to do with our need to obey the requirement of Jesus that we love them.

Nor is loving our enemies inseparable from disapproving of their opinions or conduct. It is possible that without actually liking another man we may appreciate his skill and devotion, recognize that he is making a valuable contribution to the common life, and hence in the deepest sense "approve of him." But to love one's enemy does not require even this, and the probability is large that our enemy will be someone of whom we actively disapprove. A Communist, a dishonest politician, the proprietor of a race track, the manager of a saloon, the owner of a house of prostitution—to assume that we must approve of such a person in order to love him would reduce the words of Jesus to absurdity, and whatever else may be involved in loving our enemies, we are certainly not called upon to minimize the distinctions between right and wrong which set one man against another and summon Christian people to a life of warfare in God's service.

And hence it needs to be understood that to love the enemy does not necessarily mean submitting to the enemy. Henry Hazlitt has written a sharp satire on "man-eating by tigers."

Johnny was walking through the woods on a lovely day. Suddenly a tiger sprang out of the underbrush and leaped at his throat.

It was at this point that Johnny composed his great essay on the folly of fighting tigers. Continuous warfare between men and tigers, he pointed out, serves no constructive purpose whatever, and only can lead, in time, to the destruction of one side or the other. His essay emphasized the seamy aspect of this warfare. . . . With bitter satire he ridiculed the belligerent instincts of men and tigers, and the war hysteria whipped up by antitiger propaganda. . . .

The tiger was now upon him. But Johnny disdained to retaliate under any trumped-up excuse of "self-defense." He urged, instead, a new peace conference. . . .

Unfortunately, Johnny was not given time to put these thoughts into permanent form. He had barely completed the essay in his mind when the tiger's fangs closed on his throat.[1]

There is sufficient fallacy in Hazlitt's words to keep us from swallowing them whole, but there is also enough truth to make it wrong for us to scorn them. Turning the other cheek and going the second mile do not mean resigning oneself to the triumph of evil, throwing up one's hands in easy defeat, and feeling that in surrender to what God abhors we have done what God wants. It may be that we are meant to be fools for Christ's sake, but surely we are not intended to be simply fools. It may be that we are meant to be pacifists in the sense that we are makers of peace, but certainly we are not intended to be passivists in the sense that we do nothing. It may be that we are meant to refrain from hating one who is evil, but definitely we are not intended to refrain from opposing him with a different power—doing good to the man who hates us, praying for the person who persecutes us, overcoming the wrong with the right. Loving the enemy does not necessarily mean submitting to the enemy. It does not mean blandly acquiescing while the enemy treats us in a way which corrupts his own soul and thwarts the will of God both for him and for us.

II

So much for the negative. What now about the positive aspects of the problem? Thus far we have been thinking about some of the attitudes which loving the enemy does *not* involve. Let us

[1] From "Man-Eating by Tigers Is Silly, But They Will Go On Doing It!" in *The Saturday Evening Post*, June 10, 1950. Used by permission of the author.

think next about some of the steps which loving the enemy *does* entail.

First, then, when we love our enemies, we utterly repudiate hatred and malice in our thoughts about them. Whether we like them or dislike them, whether we approve of them or disapprove of them, whether we submit to them or resist them, whether our injury from them is small and transient or deep and abiding— there is no place in love for ill will, the desire to hurt, or delight in destroying.

It would be futile to claim that even this phase of loving our enemies is simple or easy. Bliss Perry writes that one day he and some other boys asked their Sunday school teacher about the Bible verse, "As much as lieth in you, live peaceably with all men." The teacher had been fluently expounding the doctrine of nonresistance, but one of the boys was not satisfied. "Suppose the other fellow keeps pitching on you all the time?" he asked. "Well," the teacher replied, "I suppose sometimes it just doesn't lie in you."

But Eric Hoffer speaks the needed word when he says, "We are made kind by being kind." The ability to love our enemies is acquired like any other skill. We learn to love by loving, and before we do anything else in our relationships with the people whom we disapprove and oppose, we are called upon by this commandment of Jesus to banish hatred from our attitudes toward them. One by one, step by step, and day by day, we are summoned to practice doing what we do not yet know how to do. We are to learn how to drive out ill will by eliminating it from this specific word, this particular intention, this individual act.

Second, when we love our enemies, we recognize who our enemies actually are. Outside a maternity ward in Chicago two men struck up a conversation and made a startling discovery: they lived on the same street and their expectant wives were sisters who had not met for twenty-five years. And a discovery like that is inherent in the love of our enemies. With our minds we know that

God is the Father of all men, that he created everybody, and that our enemies are hence our brothers. Every war is a civil war, and when we love our enemies, we have discovered this fact not only with our minds but also with our hearts.

Thomas Hardy has given this experience a poignant description in his poem about two soldiers meeting on the battlefield:

> "Had he and I but met
>   By some old ancient inn,
> We should have sat us down to wet
>   Right many a nipperkin!
>
> "But ranged as infantry,
>   And staring face to face,
> I shot at him as he at me,
>   And killed him in his place.
>
> "I shot him dead because—
>   Because he was my foe,
> Just so: my foe of course he was;
>   That's clear enough; although
>
> "He thought he'd 'list, perhaps,
>   Offhand like—just as I—
> Was out of work—had sold his traps—
>   No other reason why.
>
> "Yes; quaint and curious war is!
>   You shoot a fellow down
> You'd treat if met where any bar is,
>   Or help to half-a-crown." [2]

Loving the enemy requires that we make Hardy's discovery

[2] "The Man He Killed." Used by permission of The Macmillan Company and The Macmillan Company of Canada, Ltd.

before we make Hardy's mistake. It means achieving the victory which Caroline Stickney suggests in "A Daughter of the Puritans." Whenever she and her sister quarreled, their mother would place them in two chairs, facing each other, and bid them to look straight into each other's eyes and on no account to smile. Very soon smiles and then laughter came, and the bad feelings were gone. Loving the enemy demands that we really see the enemy—see him as a child of God like ourselves, see him as our brother, see him as a member of our own family.

Third, loving our enemies requires understanding our enemies. Think, for example, about the young Abraham Lincoln as the best people of his time must have seen him. Here was an awkward and ungainly man whose pants were generally five inches too short for his legs, who seldom had more than one suspender, and who frequently wore neither vest nor coat. He was subject to unpredictable fits of depression, and many of his friends often thought him mad. On at least one occasion he himself consulted an eminent medical man in hope of saving his sanity, and more than once the people who lived with him removed all knives and razors from his reach lest he commit suicide. He was famous for the telling of stories which charitable people called vulgar and less tactful people labeled unclean. At last he became engaged to a lovely and accomplished girl, and on the wedding day the large company of distinguished guests gathered at the appointed place only to turn away disappointed; the groom did not appear.

See no more of Lincoln than such words as these reveal, and you might find it hard to love him. You would know his fears but not his dreams, his weakness but not his strength, the common clay with which God fashioned him but not the new and mighty spirit struggling to be born in him.

We shall not love the people whom we do not like until we understand them—know the origins from which they came, recognize the pressures which have bent and twisted them, discern the secret burdens which have sapped their strength and objectivity, appreciate the fear and guilt and hope which make them what they are.

And then, fourth, it is a part of loving our enemies that we actively seek their welfare. This does not mean helping the burglar rob a bank, giving the drunken driver another automobile in which to do more damage, or raising no objection when a nation, race, or individual is persecuted. But neither does it mean demanding that our enemy be lovable before we love him. Alan Paton has said that "he who waits until the time is ripe often waits until it is rotten," and loving our enemy requires that we seize the initiative ourselves, discover what God intends that our enemy should be or have or do, and then help him to obey God's will or receive God's blessing or become God's helper.

Arrogance is a sign not so much of strength as of weakness, and when we love an arrogant man, we help him find enough strength to be humble. Dishonesty is not so much an evidence of malice as of insecurity, and when we love a dishonest man, we welcome him to friendship which restores his confidence. Cruelty, vindictiveness, lust, greed—the qualities which we dislike in our enemies are not beings in themselves, something which can be stamped out with a heavy boot, or pierced with a knife, or killed with a gun. These are simply the words with which we describe the particular twist which has been given to a personality or the special stain which has been imposed on a life. Our enemy does not want to be a stained or twisted individual, and he suffers from his handicap far more than anyone whom he injures. The likelihood is great that he hates himself with much steadier intensity than that of anybody else who hates him, and when we love him, we thrust our way through his ugly corrosions, ally ourselves with the God-created soul within, and try to steady the weak and blinded spirit as he struggles upward into strength and light.

There are five levels of life, Gabriel R. Mason has written:

On the first level men say, "We hate you and we'll kill you." That's extermination. On the second they say, "We hate you, but we'll use you." That's exploitation. On the third they say, "We don't like you, but we'll let you alone." That's toleration. On the fourth they say, "You're different, but we know your worth." That's appreciation. On the fifth and highest level they say, "We appreciate you and will help you to realize all your latent powers and capacities." That's development.

It is also what we mean by love and especially the love of our enemies.

III

But what motive do we have for a life of this kind? There is incredible self-denial in Christian love of the enemy. There is interminable patience. There are sacrifice, humiliation, pain, and perhaps even death. And why should any reasonable man subject himself to such suffering when he is not forced to undertake it? Why not ignore our enemy, if that is possible, and destroy him if we cannot ignore him?

There are at least three sound motives for loving our enemies, and the first of them is simple decency. It is highly probable that there are those who find us as unattractive as we have found our enemies, and if our enemies have fallen short of the glory of God, could not the same be said of us? Wishing to be judged ourselves not solely in terms of our achievements but also in terms of our intentions and our handicaps, have we any reason not to use the same standards in the judgment of our enemies? Seeing a man with a sick body, we do not shoot him, and why should we treat differently a man with a sick soul? Let a man be crippled by paralysis, and his infirmity commands a double measure of our helpfulness; and why should we treat differently the person crippled by ignorance, guilt, or fear? So the first motive for loving our enemies is simple decency.

The second is more important: Jesus commands that we love them. "Love your enemies," he said. His words are clear and unmistakable, and unless the central claim of Christianity is false, the commandment of Jesus is the commandment of God. We are to love our enemies that we may be sons of the Father in heaven who makes his sun rise on the evil and on the good, and sends his rain on the just and on the unjust. We are to love our enemies that we may be "perfect" as our heavenly Father is perfect. In any realistic approach to the problem these commandments of Jesus put an end to objection. If a given act or attitude is known to be the will of God, there is no reasonable alternative to obedience. It is not significant that we fail to understand God's purposes. It is not important that we question God's wisdom. And it does not matter that we find the task forbidding and repulsive. Unless Jesus was a fraud, he comes to us as God's ambassador and faithfully reports God's will to us, and refusing to love our enemies becomes something more than disobedience to a single commandment: it becomes a repudiation of Jesus and a defiance of God which thoughtful Christians cannot find other than intolerable.

The third motive for loving our enemies grows out of the second: there is no other way of doing what needs to be done. A man goes to the dentist not because he enjoys the dentist's drill but only because there is no other way of keeping his teeth in good condition. A woman practices scales on the piano not because she takes delight in the repetition of the unmelodious measures but only because there is no other way of learning to play the piano. And we love our enemies not because we find the endeavor initially pleasant but because there is no other way of establishing justice, building peace, and making earth the fair and goodly land which God intended it to be.

If God himself is not mocked, neither does he make fools of his creatures, and he never imposes upon anyone a commandment which is impossible, unnecessary, unwise, or absurd. We are to love our enemies because God commands us to love them, but taking up the unwanted task, we are never to doubt that God would not ask it of us if it were not his only means of doing what needs to be done both for our enemies and for ourselves. There are some things which not even God can do, and when he finds us attempting to reach love on the highways of hatred, we must appear to him like the three-year-old Ethel Roosevelt clamoring to be allowed to "pick strawberries from the cherry tree." On the level of hatred if someone "wins," someone else always loses, and it is not the will of God that any of his creatures lose. A. E. Housman writes about "the sword that will not save," and God knows that the sword was never meant for the tool bags of the healers and the builders. A former chief of staff in the Royal Air Force has said that only the long-range bombing plane can prevent World War III, but God is not naïve enough to believe that "security for half the world can be achieved by creating a sense of insecurity in the other half, and that nations can get what they want most by preparing for what they want least."

Who ever heard of hatred building an enduring home, a worthy friendship, a happy neighborhood, a sound economy, or a stable nation? And what cause have we to think that motives which have failed on every other level of human relationships will be successful when we widen our horizons to embrace the world? Said Habakkuk:

> Woe to him who builds a town with blood,
> and founds a city on iniquity!

Woe, indeed; for he builds his town on shifting sand and founds his city on an evil dream. Far from being the impractical idealism which many people think, the commandment to love our enemies is the only realistic choice before us. If we do not love them because we want to, we shall love them at last because we have to. There is no other answer to evil. There is no other alternative to chaos.

Chapter VI

DO NOT BE ANXIOUS

Therefore do not be anxious, saying, "What shall we eat?" or "What shall we drink?" or "What shall we wear?" For the Gentiles seek all these things; and your heavenly Father knows that you need them all.   MATT. 6:31-32

"THE FRETFUL STIR UNPROFITABLE." THAT PHRASE BELONGS TO WILLIAM Wordsworth, and the date is July 13, 1798. On one of his tours the poet had gone back to the banks of his beloved River Wye, and thinking of what that stream had meant to him through the years, he wrote these lines:

> . . . how oft—
> In darkness and amid the many shapes
> Of joyless daylight; when the fretful stir
> Unprofitable, and the fever of the world,
> Have hung upon the beatings of my heart—
> How often has my spirit turned to thee,
> O sylvan Wye! thou wanderer thro' the woods,
> How often has my spirit turned to thee![1]

"The fretful stir unprofitable." How earnestly we wish that we might avoid it! How persistently we try to free ourselves from its bondage! How guilty we feel when we read the simple commandment of Jesus, "Do not be anxious!" and then confess to ourselves how hard it is for us to obey it.

The stomach ulcer has been called "the wound stripe of civiliza-

[1] From "Lines Composed a Few Miles Above Tintern Abbey."

tion," and so much of modern life falls within the category of experiences out of which ulcers might reasonably come. There is so much fruitless haste. There is so much anxious frustration. There is so much fretful stir which is unprofitable because it reaches no goal and achieves no purpose.

I

Of course, any attempt to deal with this unprofitable fretfulness begins in the awareness that there is nothing new either in the problems which we face or in the perplexity we often feel as we confront them. Strickland Gillilan's brief poem "On the Antiquity of Microbes" says almost everything which really needs to be said on the matter:

Adam
Had 'em.

There has always been more to be done than any man could ever do —more words to be spoken, more books to be read, more errands to be run, more blows to be struck. All religious truths are doubtable, always have been doubtable, and always will be doubtable; and no one in the years from Abraham to Jesus or from Jesus to the present moment ever lived unburdened with the same uncertainties which we are facing now. Whatever good has been wrought in the world has always been done by people often frustrated, nervous, not seeing eye to eye with friends or relatives, and hampered by bad stomachs, vengeful gall bladders, aching heads, deficient hearing, or other ills of which the flesh is frequently the heir. Evil has always seemed more powerful than righteousness. Yesterday has always seemed more holy than today. And men have always found the grass a little greener in the other fellow's yard.

People, then, have never been wholly free from fretfulness, nor should they ever hope to win such freedom. There is too much unfinished business in the world, too much injustice, too great a host of places where a little more concern might find the answer to dilemmas causing pain and heartache; and a fretful stir can often be no more than the sign that man has risen higher than the level of the dog asleep before the warming fire. But we only do ourselves damage when we add to our fretfulness the fact that our fretfulness becomes another reason for being fretful. Struggle, perplexity, and defeat are inescapable and normal aspects of our human life, and the first step toward the control of the fretful stir unprofitable is placing many of our imperfections and frustrations in the same category with the hardness of rocks and the saltiness of oceans. This is just the way God made the universe, and life can never be lived on any other terms.

II

In the second place, some of our unprofitable frustrations come from the fact that we have chosen the wrong roads for our journeying, the wrong hills for our climbing, the wrong goals for our seeking.

One summer in Colorado we grew weary of the scenic glories and synthetic attractions commonly designated as the proper substance of the tourist's day, and we fell into the habit of seeking out roads too rough for the casual traveler and with no knowledge of where they would lead us, following them as far as we could. So it happened that we often drove up into the lonely hills or out to the gold mines and the coal fields, and there finding a narrow dirt lane, we would embark upon our new adventure. But over and over again we found ourselves at last against a sheer wall of impassability. For miles we had followed a winding track through the forests while it grew narrower and narrower and narrower only to discover that it stopped on the edge of some secluded valley to which no descent could be made except by dropping over a cliff, or the road which we had chosen would fade out in a tangle of trees which looked as if they had always stood right there in the middle of what should have been the further progress of the road. Somebody had built those roads. Somebody had put a great deal of thinking and planning and toiling into their construction, and once they had probably been useful, needed, valued. But now they went nowhere. Now they were dead-end streets. Now they were of interest only to the determined wanderer or local historian, and he was doomed to nothing but discouragement who thought that he could get anywhere by following them.

It might be said of many of us that most of the roads we daily travel fit that description. "Do not be anxious . . . ," Jesus said. "But seek first [God's] kingdom and his righteousness." Yet so much of our time is spent in the nurture of self-esteem. So much of our energy is consumed in the struggle for places of preference. So many of our hungers are for the popular symbols of security— money, fine clothing, imposing houses, impressive friends. And in the perspective of eternity these are the wrong roads for our journeying. They always leave us frustrated and fretful. They are dead-end streets. They don't take us where we want to go.

When Frederick Thorne Rider, one of the lay secretaries of the Pope, gave a new building to the University of Perugia, he so gratified the Italian government that it made him a count. Edgar J. Goodspeed was at one time his next-door neighbor, and he delighted to address him with his new title. The Count always demurred, however. "I am only an ordinary man," he would say. But Goodspeed would not have it so. "By no means!" he said. "As a count, you are the real article, but as an ordinary man, Count, you are an imposter!" [2]

As children of God, loving God with all of our being and loving

[2] *As I Remember* (New York: Harper & Brothers, 1953), pp. 288-89.

our neighbor as ourselves, we are the real thing, but as greedy, grasping animals we are imposters. We are leading lives which were not meant for us; and walking the roads which lead us nowhere, we should not be surprised to find our fretful stir unprofitable. For we need to lose our lives to live them.

III

In the third place, it needs to be said that the abundant life does not depend so much upon the quantity of our activities as upon the quality. We do not need to read *everything* in order to be educated. We do not need to know *everything* in order to be wise. We do not need to see *everything* in order to be happy. We do not need to do *everything* in order to find our life's fulfillment.

Henry Drummond has written:

The world is a sphinx. It is a vast riddle—an unfathomable mystery; and on every side there is temptation to questioning. In every leaf, in every cell of every leaf, there are a hundred problems. There are ten good years of a man's life in investigating what is in a leaf, and there are five good years more in investigating the things that are in the things that are in the leaf. God has planned the world to incite men to intellectual activity.[3]

But before these incitements to intellectual—or political, or economic, or moral, or ecclesiastical—activity many a man reacts like the law student who entered a University of Oklahoma classroom to undergo his final examination, took one look at the questions, and fainted.

Yet beyond the obvious and minimal requirements with regard to bulk it should be clear to all of us that effectiveness in living does not depend so much on the quantity of our consumption as on the

[3] *Henry Drummond: An Anthology*, ed. James W. Kennedy (New York: Harper & Brothers, 1953), p. 105.

quality. We do not have to eat all the beef in the world in order to be nourished, nor all the spinach, nor all the orange juice. In fact, when we try to eat too much, we get nothing but indigestion, and we learn at last the wisdom to use restraint in what we eat, to pick from the vast opportunities open to us that which is good and right *for us*. And we find that choosing wisely and with proper discipline we are strengthened and renewed.

So, too, in the realms of the spirit. Wordsworth can feed our souls, but Tennyson can feed them also—or Shakespeare, or T. S. Eliot, or Emily Dickinson. We can find spiritual sustenance in Amos, but we can find it also in Hosea, or Micah, or Jeremiah, or Paul. It is possible that the reading of too many books will not increase a man's education but diminish it. Too much travel can contribute less to the breadth of a man's life than it takes away from the depth. Too many friends can make a man not more familiar with the wonder of the human soul but less. What is needed is the time and the will to digest our experiences, to relate them to knowledge already possessed, and to make of them the means whereby one's own particular strength and insight are turned into channels of blessing in one's life among his fellows.

Man's progress from polygamy to monogamy is evidence among other things of his discovery that having one woman as his wife, he has all women, and that striving to have many women, he does not even have one. In the areas of life's deepest significance most of us already see everything, have everything and know everything which we need to live the life of joy and peace upon the earth, and one of the reasons why we find ourselves so often in the fretful stir unprofitable is our blindness to the obvious and the immediate.

IV

And then, fourth, it must not be forgotten that even as we often do more harm in the world than we know, so, too, we often do more good. It has been said that whoever works for the good will never be unemployed, and it ought to be said also that whoever works for the good with honest commitment and reasonable intelligence will never be ineffective. The labor of the earnest and humble Christian is never in vain in the Lord. It is more significant than he understands. It is more essential to God's purpose than he ever dreams.

The illustrations are so numerous that they flood the mind beyond control. I grew up, for example, under the pastoral care of a Baptist minister in Somerville, Massachusetts. For fifteen years or more he presided over the church while I was passing from childhood into manhood, and in the natural impatience of adolescence I often thought him incredibly conservative and lacking in daring. But it was he who sent me into the ministry myself, and walking as best I could the road he walked before, I have found him still a blessed light upon my onward way. But he never knew what he had done for me: he died before I found it out myself.

For seven years I walked up to the altar of my former church in Lexington, Massachusetts, to receive the morning offering at our Sunday services, and for seven years as I faced the altar with the offering plates while the doxology was being sung, I did something which no one knew about except myself. In our order of worship the offering was followed immediately by the sermon, and standing there before the altar, I looked at the flowers, searched out some blossom lifting up its spreading petals toward the heavens, and made its symbolism mine: "Fill, O God, my heart with thy spirit and power as I preach to this congregation now." Or I found a flower bent as if it looked down toward the floor of the chancel, and I let that flower be the vehicle of my prayer for that day: "Forgive, O God, the blindness, the weakness, and the sins of mine which will make this sermon frailer than it ought to be, and do thou for this people through thine own power that which I can never do." But for seven years the flower committee of the church never knew what

THE HARD COMMANDS OF JESUS

good it did me through the flowers which it placed upon the altar Sunday after Sunday; I never thought to tell anybody.

The occasional snobbery of "educated" and "important" people is always unjustified, and some of the best educated and most important people are wholly "uneducated" and utterly "unimportant." The waitress holding in her head the complicated orders of a half dozen people and gathering up in her hands the dishes of a table for four so that a weary mother may have the uncommon treat of "eating out" that night. The fisherman lowering his incredible maze of nets into the sea and raising his catch from the bottom with such skill that the nets can be emptied in minutes and lowered back to the sea again to bring up food for his fellows to eat. The housewife blending her ingredients into a mass of dough which on being drawn forth from the oven is bread or cake to keep her sons and daughters healthy. How often have I looked upon such common tasks as these and found them uncommon, how often thought about the "uneducated" people who performed them and seen that they were far better educated than I, how often remembered that while the world could probably get along very well without my contribution to it, there would soon be chaos without the unheralded services of the multitudes of highly educated "uneducated" men and women who made my life possible.

Such service to our fellows has proper place in

> . . . that best portion of a good man's life,
> His little, nameless, unremembered acts
> Of kindness and of love.[4]

But it has an even wider meaning too; for it reaches up to touch the very throne of God. "As you did it to one of the least of these my brethren, you did it to me," Jesus warned that the King would

[4] William Wordsworth, "Lines Composed a Few Miles Above Tintern Abbey."

say on the day of judgment, and less of our fretful stir would be unprofitable if once we understood that any act of goodness which we do for anyone upon the earth is also done for God and ranks no lower in God's sight than the work of ministers at altars—and often higher.

V

Finally, there would be less anxiety in the world if we had a greater awareness of God's providence and a quicker readiness to trust it. There are many "accidents" which are not accidents, and there are many "tragedies" which are not tragedies. Things apparent are not always things real. The scorn of today is sometimes purified to become the thunderous applause of tomorrow, and the loss of a battle does not always involve the loss of a war. Man's judgment is not always God's judgment, and even as the foolishness of God is wiser than men, so is the weakness of God stronger than men.

When Dwight L. Moody went to Scotland, Henry Drummond took part in his mission, and Moody wanted Drummond to return to America with him as a member of his team. Drummond, however, had not finished his education, and there was a great struggle in his mind with regard to his true calling under God. One day while he was visiting in the lovely Highland hills in the north of Perthshire, he stumbled over a stone and wrenched his knee, and during two weeks of enforced rest he made up his mind: he would return to New College to finish his training. "A fortunate accident," most of us would say, but years later Drummond wrote to his friend Robert Barbour the following words: "I should like to make a pilgrimage to that stone. . . . Sometimes I think I owe more to it than I know. Perhaps if it had not been for that stone I should not be at college this winter." [5] And who can surely say that there was not

[5] *Op. cit.,* pp. 29-30.

in the wrenching of Drummond's knee something more than just "a fortunate accident"?

Charles Dickens was a frail child. He could not play the rough games of his contemporaries, and he spent many a lonely hour with nothing but books as his companions while the other children were enjoying their more normal pursuits together. "Poor Charles Dickens!" we say. But was this loneliness of childhood a part of the price of *David Copperfield*, the *Pickwick Papers, Little Dorrit, A Christmas Carol;* and was that loneliness too high a price to pay; and could it be that there was more in Dickens' early frailty than blind and senseless chance?

Donald Harrington points out that in his younger days Abraham Lincoln had all the characteristics of a first-class neurotic. "He was often depressed. He had black moods. He was up and then he was down." He was a lonesome person ridden by feelings of guilt, and he had a way of withdrawing into himself so that he became oblivious to everything going on around him.

But the magnificence of Lincoln may very well be due precisely to the fact that he had these troubles. All during his youth he wrestled with them and with himself. The result was that when later he was called on to face crises that were so great that his country was poised upon a precipice, he had the understanding, the patience, the courage and the stamina to stand up to those problems."

And will you say that Lincoln's preparation was the work of nothing but animal heredity or impersonal fate?

There is a power in the world which is not our own power. There is a will in the world which is not our own will. There is a victory in the world which does not depend upon our own shrewdness or even upon our own goodness. God still exists. God still is not mocked. God is still our refuge and our strength, and still we need not fear though the earth be removed and though the mountains be carried into the midst of the sea. "Do not be anxious," Jesus said, and of all the bulwarks of trust when the tides of the fretful stir unprofitable roar in upon the beaches of our souls the greatest is that providence of God which Paul described when he said, "If we live, we live to the Lord, and if we die, we die to the Lord; so then, whether we live or whether we die, we are the Lord's."

Chapter VII

BELIEF IN ME

Let not your hearts be troubled; believe in God, believe also
in me. JOHN 14:1

BELIEF IN CHRIST INVOLVES MUCH MORE THAN INTELLECTUAL ASSENT
to the claim that he was distinctively God's Son, but the full commitment of life which authentic belief entails is impossible without
the intellectual assent. We do not set sail in a boat which we suspect
to be unsafe, and before we trust a doctor's prescriptions, we demand to know something about his credentials.

The acquiescence of the mind is therefore not unimportant when
we set out to believe in Christ, and for the securing of such an acceptance of him much greater effort is required than many men
have thought. In one sense, belief in Christ is a gift, but in another,
it is a gift which only the prepared can receive. The man who wants
to believe must set out to discover the truth. He must steel himself
to accept whatever facts he finds. He must sift the evidence, re-
solve the apparent contradictions, and refuse to repudiate conclusions
which point inescapably toward a revolution in his life for which
he feels that he is far from ready.

When Jesus commanded his disciples to "believe" in him, he
was not asking for passive acceptance. Already he was calling for
action. Already he was directing them to take the little leaps of
faith which were commitments in themselves and which would
lead his disciples inexorably toward the point from which the one
great leap could be initiated. And the nineteen centuries between
his day and ours have not dulled the point of his command.

What, then, is the case for Christ's peculiar sonship? What right has he to claim our unreserved devotion? Why should we believe in him?

I

Belief in Christ is not primarily based upon the fact that he was good. Admittedly he was, but others have been good before and after him. It would be difficult and indeed impossible to pour out the character of Socrates into one bottle and that of Jesus into another and then holding them both up to the light determine which had more of moral stature in it. And even if at last we could decide that Jesus was the best man who ever lived, that discovery would not by itself give proof that he was divine. It would only show that he was good.

Nor do we believe in Christ because he was a great moral teacher. Admittedly again he *was,* but so have others been before and after him. And even if you have no doubt that Jesus' teachings are the noblest men have ever known, you still have said no more than that he was a man of deep perception and tremendous insight.

Nor do we believe that Jesus was divine because he was born of a virgin. It is wholly possible that if God willed to do so he could arrange such a birth for anyone, divine or human, and even if the virgin birth could be completely proved it would not in any sense be synonymous with divinity. But the virgin birth cannot be proved, nor even shown to be a major article of early Christian faith. In the New Testament writings all notice of the matter is confined to incidental references concerned with Joseph and Mary, and, in the early preaching, virginity in Mary is never made the proof of divinity in Christ. Indeed, the disciples seem to have forgotten this portion of the birth narratives, to regard it as utterly inconsequential, or never to have heard it at all. Contradiction and confusion are easily discernible in the few sentences still preserved about it, and any case for Christ's divinity which has no surer ground than his virgin birth is a tottering case that is doomed to be lost.

71

Still further, we do not believe that Jesus was divine because he could perform miracles. The pages of the Bible are full of similar claims for lesser men, and both the Old and New Testaments can offer countless instances where other individuals have matched or exceeded the wonderful deeds which Jesus did. Healing "miracles" are done today by people making no claim to divinity, and the fact that Jesus himself possessed such unusual powers could prove him great without proving him divine.

Even his death on the cross does not make Jesus uniquely God's son. It was a noble death, a courageous death, a selfless death, a death washed clean of bitterness and hatred and the hunger for revenge. Jesus' life was freely offered as a means of saving sinners, and the wonder of his love for men remains to most of us a beacon far beyond our reaching. But still the truth cannot be dodged that he was not the only man to suffer agony in dying, not the only man to give his life for other men, not the only man whose executioners were infinitely more guilty than the man they executed. Calvary is evidence that Jesus was brave. It is evidence that he was strong and kind and good. But of itself it does not prove that he was divine.

II

The real case for Christ's divinity begins with the clear logic of God's revelation. Ask a man to drive a nail and offer him his choice of a plane, a hammer, or a screw driver; and you would expect the man to choose the hammer. So it is with God's intent to make himself known to men. We have sometimes thought that his choice of a man as the vehicle of revelation was an incredible choice, but can we name a better one? A fish? A tree? A dog? The mountains? The stars? We ourselves are persons, and God is at least a person. What could be more clear than that when God, who is a person, sets out to communicate with men, who are also persons, he will do so in personal terms. If I believed in God but had not heard of Christ, I should at once begin to look for him; for in nothing but a person could I ever expect that the fullness of God would ever be known. God is not a system but a soul, and souls cannot be found in the charts of astronomy or the computations of geology. They have to be found in people, and once we believe in a God who wants to reveal himself to men, the presence of Christ in the world is far less strange than his absence would be.

III

There is therefore no logical barrier to belief in such a person as Christ, and one of the strongest arguments that the mantle fell upon the carpenter of Nazareth is what he said about himself. "Are you the Christ, the Son of the Blessed?" the high priest asked him at his trial, and he replied simply, "I am." But it was more than that, much more. He always taught as one whose authority came not from men but from God, and over and over again in his recorded words we find the clear conviction that he was divine as other men are not divine. "I am the way, and the truth, and the life; no one comes to the Father, but by me"—"I and the Father are one"—"I am the resurrection and the life; he who believes in me, though he die, yet shall he live, and whoever lives and believes in me shall never die"—"He who has seen me has seen the Father"—"All authority in heaven and on earth has been given to me."

It is sometimes objected that we have these words of Jesus only through the records of fallible men, that these records were not made until several decades after Jesus' own death, and that they may represent a "reading back" of later ideas into earlier times. Such protests would be far more important if the case for Christ's divinity were based upon only a few isolated statements about it, but the conviction of his peculiar relationship to God pervades all of Christ's teachings. It is the very heart of all he said and did, and we cannot pull out the heart without killing the whole. I believe that Jesus was the Christ because the best records we have report him saying that he was or assuming that he was, because those records are so constant in their testimony, and because to those who knew him best he seemed to be a man who might make such claims for himself without being either ridiculous or blasphemous.

IV

It is against the background of Jesus' own claims to be the Christ that his character and mental competence become important. There are too many arrogant people who act as if they thought they were God today, and there are plenty of deranged people who actually make that claim for themselves. But Jesus was neither arrogant nor deranged, and Charles R. Brown has clearly put the choice before us in quoting the following words:

It seems easier for a good man to believe that in a world where we are encompassed by mysteries, where man's own being itself is a consummate mystery, the Moral Author of the wonders around us should for great moral purposes have taken to himself a created form, than that the one human life which realizes the ideal of humanity, the one Man who is at once perfect strength and perfect tenderness, the one Pattern of our race in whom its virtues are combined and its vices eliminated should have been guilty, when speaking of himself, of an arrogance, of a self-seeking, and of an insincerity, which, if admitted, must justly degrade him far below the moral level of millions among his unhonored worshipers.[1]

Isolated from his own assumption of divinity, Jesus' character is inconclusive, but in conjunction with his claims to distinctive sonship it becomes another reason for believing him divine. Claiming to be Christ, he was certainly Christlike.

V

But it is not simply what Jesus said about himself that matters to us now. It is also what the ones who knew him said about him, and the ones who knew him best

[1] From *The Main Points*. Used by permission of Pilgrim Press.

believed with flaming faith that he was the Christ. . . . Those who lived
most intimately with him stood most in awe of him, with mingled love
and adoration acknowledged in him a divine authority, felt in him
the very presence of their God, gave him the supreme name they knew
to express transcendent greatness, Messiah, and after Calvary they were
victoriously confirmed in their adoration of him by their faith in his
resurrection and their experience of his living presence.[2]

These were not uninformed strangers who held those beliefs.
They were not prejudiced relatives. They were not wide-eyed
fanatics. They were sober-minded fishermen and farmers. They
were men who knew of Jesus all there was to know—his father and
mother, his brothers and his sisters, his work in the carpenter shop
before his ministry began, the things he said and did while fishing
in the lake, or walking along the hot and dusty roads, or talking to
the crowds, or sitting with a few of them upon a lonely mountain-
side. They were men whose bonds with him were not the unavoidable ties of blood and family but the voluntary ones of friendship
and love. They said that Jesus was in truth the Christ, and we have no
reason to believe that they were other than honest men. We have no
reason to conclude that they did not tell the truth.

VI

And this brings us to the Christian church. These sober-minded
fishermen and farmers, these men who knew of Jesus all there was
to know, these men whose ties with him were those of friendship
and love, these men who said that Jesus was the Christ—they sealed
their faith with their lives. The church did not begin with the affirmation that Jesus was a good man or even that he died on the
cross to save a sinning world. It began with the preaching that he
rose from the dead. It began with the gospel that he was the Son of
God. The church's one foundation was not Jesus, the carpenter of
Nazareth: it was Jesus, the Christ and the Lord, the Messiah, the

[2] H. E. Fosdick, *The Man from Nazareth* (New York: Harper & Bros., 1949).

Son of God. Johannes Weiss has rightly said that there is more evidence for the divinity and resurrection of Christ than there is for his birth or his death; for the evidence in support of Christ's divinity is all of Christianity, the entire history of the Christian church through nineteen centuries of life and labor, the world-wide incarnation of the Christian faith today.

"If Christ has not been raised," said Paul, "your faith is futile." And so it truly is. If Jesus was not really divine, Stephen's faith was vain, and his stoning had no meaning. If Jesus was not really divine, Peter's faith was vain, and his crucifixion was without significance. If Jesus was not really divine, Paul's faith was vain, and his head was chopped off to no purpose. The martyrdoms of every age and every nation, the missionary efforts all the way from Jesus to the present time, the church-founded hospitals and schools and social service centers, the humble allegiance of countless millions of obedient and faithful Christians—all of them are vain if Jesus was not truly Christ because they all were founded on the faith that he was.

But it is incredible that all these witnesses should have been mistaken. Leslie Weatherhead asks:

If he was an ordinary man, why, nineteen centuries afterward, are men writing books about him? Do you think the saints of God, dying for their faith through centuries of persecution are all deluded? Is Christian experience which issues in changed lives and heroic enterprises a form of insanity? Is all the work of the Christian church in all lands and all ages based on a dreary lie?

It *is* not so and it *cannot* be so, and the church itself is one good reason for belief in him on whom the church was founded. For how can we escape the fact that for more than nineteen hundred years the church's one foundation has been Jesus Christ her Lord?

It is not easy to believe in Jesus. On the contrary, it is inexpressibly hard. But the real source of the difficulty which we have in believing is seldom an intellectual problem, for the evidence of Christ's divinity is available to anyone, and honest doubts can finally be satisfied. It is the heart more often than the mind which proves itself the obstacle to faith. Suspecting what a transformation belief would entail in our lives, we say that we have tried to believe and cannot, when what we ought to be saying is that we are afraid to believe and will not.

Chapter VIII

CUT IT OFF

And if your hand causes you to sin, cut it off. MARK 9:43

I CAN STILL REMEMBER CLEARLY THE SUMMER I SPENT AS A THEOLOGICAL student in clinical training. Stationed in the operating room of a large general hospital, I was charged with wheeling patients into the room for their operations, returning them to their beds after the work was done, and then cleaning up the operating room for the next operation. It was never easy to watch the surgeon's knife cut into the living flesh, and many a young minister, doctor, and nurse had been known to faint at the sight. But one kind of operation seemed worse than all the others—amputations. There was something horribly final about cutting off a hand or an arm, a foot or a leg. It was like the first step in a murder, like killing a part of a human being who lay helpless to protest. You knew that when the patient waked, he would be a lesser man than when he fell asleep. You thought of crutches, mechanical limbs, the need to be helped in dressing and eating, the games no more to be played, and the hills which could never be climbed. And you longed to cry, "Stop!" to the surgeon or even to wrench the little saw out of his determined and capable hands.

It is probably a similar sense of inner rebellion which makes that strange command of Jesus so disturbing to us:

And if your hand causes you to sin, cut it off; it is better for you to enter life maimed than with two hands to go to hell, to the unquenchable fire. And if your foot causes you to sin, cut it off; it is better for you to enter life lame than with two feet to be thrown into hell. And if your eye causes you to sin, pluck it out; it is better for you to enter the kingdom of God with one eye than with two eyes to be thrown into hell, where their worm does not die, and the fire is not quenched.

Surely these are not the words of the man who loved the birds of the air and the flowers of the field. Surely not the sentiment of him who called little children to his knee and said that of such was the kingdom of heaven. They seem so harsh! They sound so brutal!

Yet how can we escape the fact that these sentences belong as surely to Jesus as any words he ever spoke? How can we avoid the obligation to thrust our way into their interior recesses, investigate their ancient caverns, and bring back into the light of day the hidden truth which all the centuries have left unchanged?

I

When such an exploration is done, the first discovery we make is that the analogy of the operating room is not wholly inept, and that in this one, strictly limited sense almost everyone already accepts the principle involved in Jesus' command. When a gall bladder is so badly diseased that it gives us no peace, we cut it out. When a vermiform appendix threatens to rupture and spread its poison into other parts of our body, we cut it out. When a hand or foot is sorely gangrenous, we cut it off, and when an eye is hopelessly infected, we pluck it out. The whole body, we say, is more important than any one of its dispensable parts, and when we cast aside the offending member, we may regret its loss, and we may be poorer without it, but we do not doubt the wisdom of removing it. At best the troublesome organ was hampering our enjoyment of life, and at worst it was threatening our very existence, and cutting it off, we bore tacit witness that there is at least one sense in which we already approve of Jesus' precept.

II

However, it takes but little further exploration to realize that the actual cutting off of a hand or a foot and the literal plucking out of an eye were not what Jesus had in mind in these words. Like every other human being, Jesus used words to hint at meanings which the words themselves can never fully convey, and every attempt at communication between one person and another must always depend upon a translation from the language of the lips or the pen to that of the mind and the heart. Jesus said that his disciples were "the salt of the earth," but no one thought he meant that they should be used as seasoning on meat. He called them "the light of the world," but no one tried to make them into lamps for his home. And when Jesus spoke of plucking out the offending eye and cutting off the tempting hand or foot, he did not have in mind an act involving knives and gouges.

After all, does the thief plot the less to steal the diamond because he has lost the hand with which to snatch it from the jeweler's window? Does the adulterer find that his lust has disappeared with the eye which once let him look upon the object of his lewdness? Does the thug become a saint when you cut off the foot with which he kicked his victim? The hand is not the real offender in stealing, nor the eye in lusting, nor the foot in beating; and trying to avoid sin by removing the bodily organs is like trying to make a little boy good by keeping him confined in a closet.

Words can never be more than symbols, and although Jesus wanted the *meaning* of his words to be followed exactly, he did not intend men so to make a fetish of the symbols that they neglected what they symbolized. Every psychiatrist has heard of mentally deranged individuals who have obeyed this commandment with verbal precision, but he knows that these people were grievously mistaken. Jesus never meant his counsel to be taken in this way, and following the letter of his law, they have lost its intent.

III

So we probe still deeper, and we discover, in the third place, that if Jesus meant nothing else by this commandment, he certainly meant that sin is indescribably serious, completely horrible, and utterly heinous.

For most of us, that evaluation of sin is not easy to accept. When we ask for a simple definition of sin, the theologians are likely to tell us that "sin is the misuse of freedom," or that "sin is anything that keeps me from God, or from being effective for God," or that "sin is the refusal of fellowship in the spirit of Christ." To the callous modern ear these definitions do not make sin sound quite so frightful as the words of Jesus imply. Bad? Yes. But not catastrophically bad!

Yet think again about that commandment: "If your hand causes you to sin, cut it off. . . . And if your foot causes you to sin, cut it off. . . . And if your eye causes you to sin, pluck it out." We have said that Jesus did not intend that his words be obeyed in literal exactness, but that does not mean that he did not intend them to be obeyed; and if sin is sufficiently serious to warrant using a figure like plucking out an eye or cutting off a hand and a foot, many of us will have to revise our ideas about it. Apparently sin is more destructive than we have imagined. The sins of violence, of course. But also the more polite and cultured sins. The sins which have washed their faces, changed their clothes, and gone to live in the big white houses on the better side of the railroad tracks. The sins of conscious omission, the sins of personal cowardice, the sins of deliberate malice.

One day in London we went out to Madame Tussaud's Wax Exhibition. Much of the display was quite ordinary—effigies of famous people looking more or less like the men and women whom they represented. But down in the simulated dungeons was a chamber of horrors. Here were the famous criminals and the crimes which they had committed. Here were the medieval tortures and the instruments which were used to inflict them. Thumb screws, leg crushers, racks, spiked wheels, and iron maidens. The iron chair and mask in which human beings were roasted alive. The iron cage in which ecclesiastical offenders were hung up on castle walls and left to starve. The torture of the hooks, in which the giant barb was thrust through the abdomen and the victim suspended in air. Prison cells, gallows, guillotines, knives, pistols, and headmen's axes.

About sins like these we have no doubt. They are too horrible even to contemplate. But most of Jesus' teaching was directed toward a different kind of sin. Sins like those which Nels Ferré had in mind when he pointed out that while sin is sometimes a conscious act, it is also sometimes a state of soul in which a man characteristically puts himself in the center of the world and makes himself the measure and end of all his striving. Sins like jealousy, competition for glory, irritability, hardness of heart, stubbornness, and the rejection of sacrifice. Unless Jesus was completely in error, these sins are sometimes even worse than those depicted by Madame Tussaud. They are serious, so serious that it is not an exaggeration to say that to avoid committing them, a man would be justified in cutting off his hand or plucking out his eye.

IV

And then, fourth, it is one of the implications of Jesus' commandment that the life to which he called his followers is the truly happy life, and like his emphasis upon the awfulness of sin, this, too, is hard for us to understand. In many minds the Christian life is a cold and brittle thing, barren of color, robbed of joy, and utterly devoid of excitement and pleasure. We think of sin like the airplane pilot who said that once when he dived 30,000 feet and all of his sins flashed vividly before his eyes, he found the experience so interesting that he went back and dived eight more times. And we think of goodness as did Henry David Thoreau when he said that if he knew for a certainty that a man was coming to his house with the conscious design of doing him good, he would run for his life.

But not so in the teaching of Jesus. Sin was to be interpreted not in terms of its shallow and ephemeral pleasures but in terms of its affront to God, its corruption of the sinner himself, and its damage to those sinned against. Goodness was to be understood not so much as self-denial but rather as self-affirmation. To be sure, you lost one life in following Jesus, but the life you gained was immeasurably grander and finer. You gave up houses and lands, but in return you received a hundredfold. The poor in spirit, the meek, the merciful, the pure in heart—in the teaching of Jesus, men and women like these were not simply faithful disciples: they were also happy people. They were fortunate, for theirs was "the kingdom of heaven." They were richly favored, for they would "inherit the earth," "obtain mercy," and "see God."

Take our desire for freedom. Sin claims to give it to us, and the sinner says that he has found it. "No restrictions for me!" the libertine cries. "I'm not going to be bound by laws and rules. I'm going to do as I please. I'm free!" But see what happens when that course is followed. He steals, and immediately his freedom is lessened. He has to disguise or conceal the article which he has stolen. He does not dare to use it openly for fear of discovery, and from the moment of his theft to the end of his days his mind will be haunted by the dread of finding out that someone saw what he did. Or he tells a lie, and immediately his freedom is circumscribed. No longer is he free to go his way in peace. Henceforth all of his words must be studied. He must be sure that everything he says conforms with the lie which he told, and adding lie to lie, he sees himself entangled at last in a spider's web of his own making, unable to escape and incapable even of hope. Or he commits adultery, and immediately his freedom is reduced. He loses the quiet trustfulness of his own family. He lives daily at the mercy of his partner in sin. Each casual remark of friend or foe must be carefully scrutinized for the hidden meaning which might reveal the knowledge of his guilty secret. And should the time ever come when he wants to stand on some unshakable ground and speak some brave word for the truth, he will always be afraid, for he will never know when someone will open his past to the world and discredit not only himself but also his cause.

It is only in goodness that true freedom is found—or power, or joy, or love—and it is one of the meanings of this commandment of Jesus that the blessings of the good life are glorious beyond our fondest dreams. They are so filled with wonder and gladness that a hand is not too high a price to pay for them, nor a foot, nor an eye.

V

In the fifth place, it is the clear word of this commandment that in any conflict of loyalties the lesser good must be sacrificed for the greater. There was no claim on Jesus' part that the hand was evil—the father's hand which earned bread for his loved ones, the mother's hand which fed her baby, the doctor's hand which stroked the fevered forehead. There was no claim on his part that the eye was evil—the artist's eye which saw a loveliness later carved into marble, the farmer's eye which led him through his daily chores, the Samaritan's eye which told him of his brother's need and pain. There was no claim on his part that the foot was evil—the little boy's foot as he played in the fields with his dog, the pilgrim's foot as he made his way up to Jerusalem, the fisherman's foot as he hurried down to his boat by the sea. The hand, the eye, the foot— these were obviously good. They were precious blessings. They were gifts from God himself. But when a greater and a lesser good were set before a man and he could not have both, how could he be wise and choose the lesser?

It is good to be comfortable, to sit on your porch in the cool of the evening and rest from the work you have done; but not when your five-year-old son is just stepping off the curb into the path of a speeding truck. It is good to live in harmony with your fellows, to live and let live, and to have no war with anyone; but not when prostitution is invading your town or dope peddlers are surrounding your high school. It is good to obey the laws of the land, to give respect to officers of government, and to maintain peace and order; but not always when the seats of power have been usurped by corrupt politicians or racial bigots or the advocates of religious persecution.

Think about the fear of peace which often looms almost as large as the fear of war in many hearts today. If the world were ever to know a firm and dependable peace, many war-supported industries would lose the major portion of their income, and most people would say that industrial prosperity is good. If peace comes, many common laborers would be out of work, and steady employment is good. If peace comes thousands of our young men would never know any education beyond high school, and a college education is good. If peace comes, many families would never see any other part of the world than the United States of America, and acquaintance with different lands and peoples is good. But is there no other way to achieve these goods? And if there is not, is it unreasonable to say that these goods must be cut off and plucked out to save the even greater good of loving our enemies, praying for those who despitefully use us, and refraining from the hating, the maiming, and the killing which war inescapably entails?

This is the truth which lies behind the words of Jesus when he said that a man ought to render to Caesar the things that are Caesar's and to God the things that are God's, or when he warned that a man who loved father or mother more than him was not worthy of him, or when he told about a merchant who found one pearl of great value and sold all that he had to buy it. Some things were more important than other things, he was saying, and when you had to make a choice, you chose the more important and not the

85

less. The soul was more important than the body; for what would it profit a man if he gained the whole world and lost his own soul? Eternal life was more important than a hand, a foot, or an eye; and if you had to choose between them, you chose eternal life.

VI

Finally, these words of Jesus are a stern reminder that in the warfare of the Christian life victory demands complete devotion. There was a sense in which those who were not against Jesus could be counted as being for him, but there was an even more important sense in which those who were not for him must be counted as being against him. Anyone who was in earnest about following him could not stop in the courtyard: he must go on to Golgotha. It was all or nothing.

The need for such complete allegiance is not so strange as we might quickly think, for a thousand steps are often made as nothing when the final step is not successfully accomplished. Here is a tiger reaching for a sleeping baby in a jungle clearing. Before coming to the jungle you practiced for weeks in preparation for just such an emergency, but you have time for only one shot, and you miss it. And you might as well never have practiced. Here is a photographer waiting for the Queen to emerge from St. Paul's. He has studied his camera for days, bought an exposure meter, jockeyed himself into perfect position, determined the focus, opened the diaphragm to the proper setting, arranged the shutter speed correctly. The Queen comes out, and he takes his pictures with joyful abandon. But when he gets home, he finds that he forgot to remove the cover from his lens. And he might as well never have bought the camera. Almost kicking the football between the goal posts, almost saving a man from suicide, almost leaping the deep and rocky chasm, almost catching the acrobatic bar above the netless circus floor—let such an issue hang in balance, and there is no compromise position. Either you wholly succeed, or you wholly fail; and defeat is just as final if measured in minutes or inches as when marked by hours or miles.

Was it not a thought like these which prompted Jesus' commandment? In the barrel of the Christian life there could not even be one bad apple because the rottenness of one would soon infect them all. If you had kept all of the commandments and lacked only one thing to qualify you as a disciple, you still could not assume discipleship until you had gained the one thing you lacked, for disloyalty in one part of a man's being could easily become disloyalty in every part. No corner of life could be held outside the pledge of allegiance. Ambition, indolence, lust, pride, temper—every knee must bow before the King or the kingdom's gates could not be opened; for the greatest of the commandments was this: "You shall love the Lord your God with *all* your heart, and with *all* your soul, and with *all* your mind." [1]

"If your hand causes you to sin, cut it off. . . . And if your foot causes you to sin, cut it off. . . . And if your eye causes you to sin, pluck it out." The words still strike the mind with shocking force, but if Henry Drummond was right in saying that most of the difficulties of trying to live the Christian life arise from attempting to half live it, this stark commandment of Jesus is not a proclamation of doom but a gospel of hope.

[1] Italics mine.

87

Chapter IX

LOVE YOURSELF

You shall love . . . yourself. MATT. 22:39

IT WAS A DEEPLY TROUBLED WOMAN WHO GAVE ME MY FIRST REAL awareness of the problem involved in loving ourselves. For years she had lived under the constant care of one of the best psychiatrists in a large midwestern city. She had spent many months in mental hospitals and many more months living at home but going back and forth each day for treatments by her psychiatric counselor in the hospital. But still she was not well, and still she never knew when, against herself and in spite of herself, she might slash her wrists with a razor blade or jump head-first into an empty bathtub.

One day she was telling me how she felt about it all, and suddenly she turned to me in perfect clarity and utter earnestness. "I have a subject for one of your sermons," she said. "Some day you ought to preach on the topic, 'Love Yourself.'" And then she told me how she distrusted herself, disliked herself, loathed herself. "If only I could love myself, I would be all right," she said. "But I can't! I hate myself!"

That is one of the principal difficulties of large numbers of people. They hate themselves, and hearing the commandment of Jesus about loving their neighbors, many of them do not even understand its implication that they ought also to love themselves.

I

Of course, there are many different forms of self-love, and it is not the adoration of the self which most people need. Not the pampering of the self. Not the indulgence of the self. It has been said that egotism and ignorance are the two basic factors in all forms of mental illness, and most people do not need any more egotism—or, for that matter, any more ignorance! A friend of mine once directed a church choir. One of the choir members was a lady named Lord who happened to be hard of hearing, and whenever the director mentioned an anthem involving "the name of the Lord," the lady would quickly look up and anxiously ask, "Did you speak to me, Mr. Jones?" Too many people daily make a similar but less justifiable confusion of themselves with the Lord, and thinking of the kind of self-love which most of us need, we do not mean setting up oneself in God's place and then bowing down before the self, praising the self, worshiping the self. For there is still a sense in which we must lose our lives to find them, and there is still a requirement that we must deny ourselves before we can fulfill ourselves.

II

Yet there is in man's selfhood something which he cannot wisely treat lightly or scorn. "You shall love your neighbor as yourself," Jesus said, and presumably he intended both aspects of that commandment to be taken seriously. Men were not only to love their neighbors: they were also to love themselves, and Jesus placed the reason for the love of the self where every man properly finds it— in God's creative purpose and action.

"In the beginning," the ancient writer said, "God created the heavens and the earth. . . . Then God said, 'Let us make man in our image, after our likeness. . . .' So God created man in his own image, in the image of God he created him." It is not good that man despise what God has created—even when the particular product of God's creation is the very man who thinks about it; for knowing that God created us "in his own image," how can we hate the creature without blaspheming the Creator?

Every man ought to cultivate a healthy objectivity about himself, and C. S. Lewis cleverly describes the end we seek in the counsel given by Screwtape, the elderly devil in hell, to Wormwood, his young nephew on the earth, as Wormwood tries to corrupt the faith of a person who is in danger of becoming a Christian:

Fix in his mind the idea that humility consists in trying to believe [his] talents to be less valuable than he believes them to be. No doubt they *are* in fact less valuable than he believes, but that is not the point. . . . By this method thousands of humans have been brought to think that humility means pretty women trying to believe they are ugly and clever men trying to believe they are fools. . . . [God] wants to bring the man to a state of mind in which he could design the best cathedral in the world, and know it to be the best, and rejoice in the fact, without being any more (or less) . . . glad at having done it than he would be if it had been done by another. [God] wants him, in the end, to be so free from any bias in his own favour that he can rejoice in his own talents as frankly and gratefully as in his neighbour's talents—or in a sunrise, an elephant, or a waterfall.[1]

Have you ever watched a dog try to cross a busy street? It darts this way and that, and wherever it goes, cars swerve or come to a stop. Nobody analyzes his reasons for taking these actions, but no one wants to run over the animal. No one wants to maim it or kill it. You might call the instinct "reverence for life," and its roots reach down to the deep, dark soil of surest truth. There is something sacred about life, any life; and if this be true of the life of a dog, then how much more of our own, we who were made in God's image and ordained to "have dominion over the fish of the sea, and over the birds of the air, and over the cattle, and over all the earth, and over every creeping thing that creeps upon the earth."

In dealing with ourselves we are not dealing with rubbish: we are dealing with jewels, and there is cause neither for vain pride

[1] *The Screwtape Letters*, pp. 72-73. Copyright 1947 by The Macmillan Company. Used by permission of The Macmillan Co. and Geoffrey Bles Ltd.

nor for false humility in such a valuation of ourselves. Each least creature on the earth is the handiwork of God, and we sing his praises for the gift of ourselves no less than for the gift of our friends and our neighbors. For the psalmist was right:

Know that the Lord is God!
It is he that made us, and we are his;
We are his people, and the sheep of his pasture.

III

Yet the right kind of self-love is not only justifiable but also deeply needed, and nowhere more than in our struggle to live with ourselves. For we are our own worst enemies.

One day, for example, we were having guests for dinner at the parsonage. It was a very special occasion, and we had imported lobsters all the way from one of the coastal islands of Maine. As I broke open the bodies, it occurred to me that our cat, Barnstable, might like some lobster, too. So I placed one of the discarded bodies on the grass outside the cellar door and set Barnstable free. It was obvious in a moment that I had not been mistaken about her appetite for lobster, and I went back inside assured that she would be busy on the grass for some time to come. But only a minute had passed when I heard a low growl behind me and found that Barnstable had picked up the lobster body, circled the house, and dropped into the cellar again through an open window. On the bench was an old mirror, and landing in front of it, Barnstable found herself face to face with what looked like another cat threatening her possession of the prized lobster. For several minutes she engaged in throaty altercation with her supposed foe, and she never found out that her enemy was no one but herself.

In an average year 22,000 people in the United States kill themselves, and 100,000 more try and fail; and the real cause for such suicidal attempts, say the psychiatrists, is "a deep sense of guilt with an unquestionable penchant for self-punishment."[2] We have not learned what G. K. Chesterton calls the great lesson of "Beauty and the Beast"—that a thing must be loved before it is lovable.[3] We have not understood the truth in Matthew Arnold's poem:

> We would have inward peace
> But will not look within.[4]

It is always right that we should want to be different from what we are in the sense that we want to be cleaner and finer, stronger and truer, braver and kinder. But it is never right that we should want to be different in the sense that I, John Smith, want to be you, Robert Jones, or that I, Helen Adams, want to be you, Mary Rogers. You may be handsome, and I may be homely. You may be brilliant, and I may be dull. You may have a placid disposition, and I may always be thinking and planning. But God made me as I am. He gave me talents of my own and opportunities of my own. He has a work for me to do in the world, and in the doing of that work you simply have no place. Your talents and your assets have no more fitness for my task than mine have for yours, and both my peace of mind and my effectiveness in God's plan depend not upon my rejecting myself, repudiating myself, hating myself, but upon my accepting myself, rejoicing in myself, using myself.

Moreover, any lasting self-improvement is always built not upon the scorn of the self but upon the love of the self. If I despise myself, then nothing is too low for me to think or say or do; but if I have a high opinion of myself, then I have splendid incapacities and lofty compulsions. If I love myself, I can neither stoop to the low temptation nor turn my back on the noble commandment. One gives garbage to pigs but not pearls, and refuse is thrown on the dump but not a baby.

[2] *Time,* August 16, 1948.
[3] *Orthodoxy,* pp. 86-87.
[4] From "Empedocles on Etna."

Shakespeare spoke the truth when he had one of his actors make the comment:

> Self-love, my liege, is not so vile a sin
> As self-neglecting.[5]

"We cannot stop caring for ourselves," writes Harry Emerson Fosdick. "We ought not to stop caring for ourselves. Our initial business in life is to care so much for ourselves that *I* tackles *Me*, determined to make out of him something worthwhile." [6] And the only adequate basis for such an effort to lift the self to loftier heights is not a low opinion of the self but a high opinion of the self, not hating the self but loving the self.

IV

Furthermore, the love of self is needed also in each man's fellowship with those around him. "You shall love your neighbor as yourself," Jesus said, and it is one of our unlearned lessons that we cannot do the former if we have not done the latter. As long as we are unfair to ourselves, unfailingly we shall be unfair to our neighbors; and as long as we hate ourselves, we cannot help hating our fellows also.

"We do not go to cowards for tender dealing," Robert Louis Stevenson once wrote; "there is nothing so cruel as panic; the man who has least fear for his own carcass, has most time to consider others." [7] Washington Irving puts the same truth in different setting. "Those who are well assured of their own standing," he writes, "are least apt to trespass on that of others; whereas nothing is so offensive as the aspirings of vulgarity, which thinks to elevate itself

[5] *Henry V*, Act II, scene 4.
[6] *On Being a Real Person*, p. 174.
[7] From "Aes Triplex."

by humiliating its neighbor." [8] And so it goes throughout the length and breadth of human living. Insecure inside, we are undependable outside. Dissatisfied with what God has made of us, we dislike what God has made of everyone else. Afraid within, we become arrogant without; and knowing that we cannot trust ourselves, sooner or later we discover that we have no capacity for trusting anybody.

During the confused days of the Boston Police strike in 1919 many public-spirited citizens were trying to find a legitimate adjustment of conflicting opinions, and Governor Coolidge was repeatedly urged to declare himself in favor of a compromise. Finally a group of friends called upon him at the State House and warned him that if he did not take that course, he would be defeated in the coming election, but his only reply was this: "It is not necessary for me to be elected."

Such integrity in public relations is not the product of self-repudiation but of self-acceptance. It is not made possible by despising the self but by exalting the self. We do not walk most surely on dunes of shifting sand. We stand with greatest confidence on rock, and our soundest competence for fellowship with other people is built upon the rock of knowledge that we are God-created souls —loved by him, wanted by him, upheld by him. For we have to be friends with ourselves before we can be friends with anybody else.

There is a haunting fantasy by Maurice Edelman about a Young Man who loved a Wicked Girl. The Young Man was wicked too, but not so wicked as the Girl. He lived with his mother, a widow, on the edge of a wood. In a flat in the town nearby the Wicked Girl lived alone, having disowned her parents, who were working-class people. No one knew how the Wicked Girl made her living, but the Young Man played pool. Every day he went into the town to call on her. Sometimes she received him, and sometimes she refused; but the Young Man lived happily except for one thing. He needed

[8] From *The Sketch Book*.

money for the Wicked Girl. So he sold his father's medals and books, various articles of furniture, and other things about the house—even his mother's wedding ring.

One cold, winter day they were talking about what the Wicked Girl wanted for Christmas, and the Young Man said that he would give her anything in the world. "Bring me a plate of peacock's brains," she commanded, and he said, "I will." "And garnish it with flamingoes' tongues." "I will," said the Young Man. "But first," she said, "you must bring me your mother's heart"; and the Young Man replied, "Even that."

It was Christmas Eve, and the snow fell heavily as the Young Man staggered through the drifts carrying his mother's heart on a platter. On the bridge by the frozen river he stumbled and fell, and the heart fell with him to the earth. And as he raised himself from the ground, a little voice came from the heart: "Are you hurt, my son? Are you hurt?" [9]

Can we remind ourselves too often that God cares for each of us with a love like that? However unlovely we may be or think ourselves to be, however greedy or lustful or cruel or ugly, God still loves us with a love which never changes. And if the self which God has given us is held so high by him who gave it, have we any other proper choice than so to love ourselves that having been created in God's image, we partake more largely of his likeness?

[9] Condensed from "Folk Tale," *New Statesman and Nation*, December 23, 1950. Used by permission.

Chapter X

TAKE UP THE CROSS

And he called to him the multitude with his disciples, and said to them, "If any man would come after me, let him deny himself and take up his cross."   Mark 8:34

HOW MANY OF THE SAYINGS OF JESUS ARE CONNECTED WITH THE experience involved when a man decides to "take up his cross." Denying the self, going the second mile, turning the other cheek, losing one's life, loving the enemy, sanctifying the self, laying down one's life for his friends—over and over again Jesus impresses on his followers the need to subdue themselves to sacrifice, and the conclusion can scarcely be avoided that an ugly instrument of execution became the holy symbol of a way of life which could not be removed from Jesus' teaching without destroying the teaching itself.

"If any man would come after me," Jesus said, "let him . . . take up his cross." It is as simple as that. You cannot get around the cross without also getting around Jesus. If you want the latter, you must take the former too.

I

What, then, do we mean by the cross? What is the way of life which lies behind it? What kind of purpose makes it meaningful today?

For one thing, any experience rightly described as a cross is never conscription. It is always voluntary enlistment. When I fall victim to infantile paralysis and am confined to my bed through weary weeks of convalescence, that experience by itself is not properly called a cross. I did not volunteer for my affliction: I was conscripted. When a tornado sweeps across my town and leaves me homeless, I am not enduring a cross. I had no choice in the matter: the tornado was "an act of God." And when a loved one dies, and I daily bear the agony of lonely memories which swiftly slip backward and of cherished hopes which will never find fulfillment, I am not carrying a cross. I did not choose to have my loved one die; she was ripped and torn from me against my will. Conscripted, we do not bear a cross but a burden; for carrying a cross, we always carry it by our own free choice.

Moreover, the cross is never mere resigned acceptance. It always involves active effort. When we use the ancient words about turning the other cheek, it is the common procedure to imagine a man abjectly groveling before his enemies and having no other motive in his nonresistance than seeking peace at any price. But this is nothing more than bitter travesty of Christian faith and teaching. Was Jesus passive in his proclamation of God's love and power? Was Paul? Were Peter, Andrew, James, and John? And what about Augustine in Africa, St. Francis at Assisi, Luther at Worms, Judson in Burma? What about the great prophets of Christian concern for education, medicine, poverty, race prejudice? Were they passive? Were they apathetic? Were they comatose? Whatever else the cross may mean, it always involves action. It requires war. It means invasion.

The cross is the denial of oneself for the sake of his fellows. The cross is Christlike love for other men. The cross is the performance in Christ's name of deeds for God's sake which are a contribution to the welfare of other people beyond the requirements of simple justice and ordinary decency.

The cross suffers long and is kind. It does not envy, does not vaunt itself, is not puffed up. It does not behave itself unseemly, does not seek its own, is not easily provoked, thinks no evil, rejoices not in iniquity but rejoices in the truth. It bears all things, believes all things, hopes all things, endures all things. Shakespeare was thinking of other matters when he wrote his famous sonnet, but still his words provide a worthy vehicle for the kind of love which we mean by the cross:

> Love is not love
> Which alters when it alteration finds,
> Or bends with the remover to remove:
> O, no! It is an ever-fixed mark,
> That looks on tempests and is never shaken;
> It is the star to every wandering bark,
> Whose worth's unknown, although his height be taken.
>
> . . . .
>
> Love alters not with his brief hours and weeks,
> But bears it out even to the edge of doom.

In the love and self-denial of the cross there are no limits either of time or of person. They include everybody, and they bear it out "even to the edge of doom."

II

It is not surprising that such a conception of God's will for men should meet resistance, and so, of course, it has. As early as the time of Paul the cross was one of the major obstacles to the acceptance of the Christian faith, and in his description of the attitudes of the Jews and the Greeks of his day there is a clear foreshadowing of the centuries which came after them.

Think first about the problem of the Jews. They found the cross a stumbling-block, Paul said, and how could we expect them to find it anything else? For centuries they had lived beneath the hated rule of foreign conquerors. The Assyrians, the Babylonians, the Persians, the Greeks, and the Romans—all these the Jews had known as their masters, and for centuries they had dreamed about the coming of the Messiah, the deliverer, the princely king whose mighty legions would put the foe to rout and usher in the day of triumph for the chosen people of the Lord. And when Jesus came, what did they find? A Nazarene, a carpenter, a man whose army numbered twelve and whose victory was execution by the very foe he came to conquer.

No wonder that the Jews found the cross to be a stumbling-block, and no wonder either that we share their difficulty today. Who ever finds it easy to love his enemies, to do good to those who hate him, and to pray for those who despitefully use him? Who ever finds it easy to clamp his pride in his pocket and to speak kindness when he longs to shout hatred? Who ever finds it easy to put the welfare of other people ahead of his own, so that he does not buy the new automobile but sends the money overseas for refugee relief or does not go on the skiing trip but makes a larger contribution to the mission boards of his denomination? Who ever finds it easy to make sacrifices for which the world thinks him stupid and to spend his time on people whom the world despises?

Or take the problem of the Gentiles. They thought the cross was foolishness, Paul said, and why shouldn't they? The Gentile Greeks were trained in reason, and they prided themselves on their wisdom. They were experienced philosophers, and they put their trust in the power of the mind to solve man's problems and to win man's salvation. Thales and Heraclitus, Xenophanes and Zeno, Plato and Aristotle—these men they knew and honored but when Jesus came, what did they find? A despised Jew, an itinerant preacher, a deranged fanatic who claimed that he and God were one.

No wonder that the Greeks thought the cross was folly, and no wonder either that it often seems no different to us today. When we think about the methods and the purposes of the Communists in their struggle for the domination of the world, is it wholly unreasonable to suspect that self-denying love would be a foolish weapon with which to confront them? When we have gone out of our way to be helpful to another person, when we have disregarded our own convenience and been unstinting of our time and effort in the attempt to bring him some deeply needed benefit, and when in

THE HARD COMMANDS OF JESUS

return he does no more than spurn our good offices and laugh at our gullibility, is it utterly beyond comprehension that we should sometimes think that we have been nothing but fools? And when we have made a sacrificial gift of money toward the support of missions in a foreign country only to read some vitriolic comment by a citizen of that country with regard to the wickedness of capitalistic America, is it completely strange that we should often wonder about the wisdom of our action?

For nineteen hundred years many people have found the cross a stumbling-block. For nineteen hundred years many people have thought the cross was foolishness. They still do; and these words of Jesus about the centrality of the cross in Christian commitment are among the most difficult and unwanted words in the whole gospel.

III

But for those who move ever deeper into Christian territory the time comes at last when they understand that they have been people "whose minds are like concrete: all mixed up and permanently set," and that theirs has been the predicament of the man who claimed that the drugstore had put the wrong labels on his two prescriptions, causing him for the past year to rub his stomach medicine on his scalp and drink his hair tonic. To those who are called, Paul said, the cross is the power of God and the wisdom of God; and sooner or later the earnest Christian discovers that Paul spoke only the truth.

In the second century after Christ there was a man named Polycarp who was bishop of Smyrna. He was eighty-six years old when they dragged him into the arena and the Roman proconsul demanded that he renounce his Christian faith. And why are we to suppose that Polycarp chose to be burned at the stake rather than speak the simple words which would have saved him? Because it was a little chilly in the town that day, and he thought the flames would warm his aged bones? Because he had a fine sense of show-manship, and he knew how pleased the crowd would be to see the spectacle?

About twelve hundred years later there was a man named John Wycliffe who translated the Scriptures into English so that the common people could read them and who formed an order of "poor preachers" to carry the gospel into every part of the land. And why are we to suppose that Wycliffe was willing to face the misunderstanding, the hatred, and the hardships which were inflicted on him and his friends? Because he hoped to retire on the royalties from his translation? Because he had a twisted personality and inwardly liked to be punished?

John Wesley often traveled more than five thousand miles a year. He preached some fifteen sermons a week. He gave away about fourteen hundred pounds every year to the poor and the needy. And why are we to suppose that he poured out his life in that manner? Because he liked horses? Because he enjoyed the sound of his own voice? Because it gave him the sense of being important?

Why did Francis turn his back on the comfortable life with which his father provided him and set out to travel the world with bare head and bare feet, begging his bread and preaching repentance? Why did Carey go to India, and Judson to Burma, and Livingstone to Africa? Why did Washington Gladden spend so many sleepless nights trying to solve the labor problems of his day? It was certainly not because Francis liked the feel of the grass on his feet when he walked around without his shoes, nor because Carey and Judson and Livingstone had an urge to be world travelers, nor because Washington Gladden found delight in the awesome sights and sounds of the slums.

Across the whole sweep of the Christian centuries there has been a strange, new motivation driving men to spend their lives as they have spent them. You might describe that motivation in terms of Albert Schweitzer, of whom it has been said that having been born into a period of pain and decay for mankind, he deliberately decided so to live that his own life would be one reply to that suffering and decadence. Or, even better, you might describe it in terms of men who saw that there was no other road to the world's salvation and, setting out to follow Jesus, took up the cross which was inseparable from discipleship in his name.

When I distrust the cross, I am daydreaming. I am making believe that the world is different from the way God actually made it. I am like the little boy who bought an old clock, indulged in a minor dismantling of its parts, put it together again, and set it going in his room. But the adjustments were not quite correct, and the family soon discovered that it was loudly striking the hours when it ought to have been striking the half-hours and vigorously announcing that the time was ten when it was really only half-past three. The clock was out of step with the universe, and even as the time of the stars was not altered by the announcements of the clock, neither is God's use of the cross changed by man's pretense that God has chosen other methods for the coming of his kingdom.

The denial of oneself for God's sake, the losing of one's life in Jesus' name, the turning of the other cheek, the walking of the second mile, the bearing of a cross—these are the power of God and the wisdom of God because there is no other way to save man from his ignorance, his folly, and his sin. If man were a thing or an animal, other methods might be used to bring him to his intended perfection in God's sight; but since man is a human being created in the image of his heavenly Father, there is no other road to his salvation but the road of the cross. If righteousness could come by the law, Christ need never have died. But it cannot come by the law: it can only come by the cross.

James S. Stewart puts the matter clearly as he uses one of T. S. Eliot's plays to interpret the power of those who bear crosses. Stewart writes:

The principle can be seen at work in the patriot suffering for his country, in the research doctor sacrificing his own health for the victims of disease, in the philanthropist wearing himself out to ransom the down-trodden and oppressed, in the captain of a sinking vessel getting the women and children to safety and then going down with his ship. The man who protests "I want no suffering for me" is ignoring the fact that not only religion but the whole of life is built that way. What Caiaphas said in cold, calculating cynicism—"It is expedient that one man should die for the people"—may be the voice of the devil, as indeed it was on Caiaphas' unscrupulous lips. But looked at from another angle, it is the very truth of God. It *is* expedient—it always has been and always will be expedient—that one man should die for the people. David Livingstone, dying on his knees in darkest Africa; the X-ray pioneer losing limb or life for the advancement of knowledge and the relief of suffering; the Headmaster of an English school who during an air-raid marshalled his pupils into the shelters and then, going back to make sure that none had been left behind, was himself caught by a bomb and instantly killed—"one man dying for the people." This is the cosmic principle of love, the cruciform pattern on which life itself is built, the ground plan of the universe.[1]

And then Stewart turns to that scene in Eliot's *Murder in the Cathedral,* where assassins come to the great church of Canterbury to kill the archbishop. When the priests attempt to bar the doors to save him, he will not have it:

> Unbar the doors! throw open the doors!
> I will not have the house of prayer, the church of Christ,
> The sanctuary, turned into a fortress.
> The Church shall be open, even to our enemies. Open the door![2]

When the priests protest that even as he would bar the door to

---

[1] *A Faith to Proclaim.* Used by permission of Chas. Scribner's Sons.
[2] Used by permission of Harcourt, Brace & Co. and Faber & Faber Ltd.

wild beasts, so he should bar it to men who "would damn themselves to beasts," the archbishop replies:

> We have fought the beast
> And have conquered. . . .
> Now is the triumph of the Cross, now
> Open the door! I command it. OPEN THE DOOR! [3]

This marks the progress, past and future, of all man's life in the
world. We have taken over earth's dominion from the wild animals
which once were its rulers. We have fought the beast and have
conquered. Now all that remains is the conquest of man himself,
and nothing will suffice for that but self-denial. Nothing will be
effective but sacrifice. Nothing will prevail but the cross.

No man can say for any other man precisely where his field of
labor ought to be, but in the providence of God no man is left without a cross to carry. Albert L. Patterson found his cross in Phenix
City, Alabama. In that wide-open town he had fought vice and
corruption for years. Liquor, gambling, and prostitution were the
debts which he charged to his account, and he was being so effective
in the payment of them that one day someone stepped up to his
car as he parked outside the building in which he had his office
and shot him to death. Not everyone who fights for civic decency
will be treated in that way or find a need as dire as that of Phenix
City, but what a clear, insistent call there is for lawyers like Patterson
who take upon themselves the helplessness of their fellows and
become themselves the means whereby the wrongs of men are
righted!

Dr. Jonas E. Salk found his cross in the crippling damage done
by infantile paralysis, and what a need there is for other scientists
who take upon their own backs the burden of man's suffering from
cancer, tuberculosis, and heart disorders! Bishop G. Bromley Oxnam
found his cross when the House Committee on Un-American

[3] *Ibid.*

104

Activities began intimating that anyone who disagreed with its methods or opinions automatically proved himself to be a Communist, and what a need there is for ministers and teachers, for legislators and politicians, who understand that all dissent is not disloyalty and that contemporary attempts to label sound reform as subversive advance the very cause they claim to oppose! Editor Mabel Norris Reese found her cross when the local sheriff declared that five children of Indian-Irish stock were really Negroes and forced their exclusion from the white public school at Mount Dora, Florida, and what a need there is for newspaper men and real estate agents, for hotel owners and travel bureau representatives, for laborers and housewives, who know that God made of one blood all of the peoples of the earth and who have no patience with the persecution of a man because of color, class, or creed!

Jesus' consecration of himself was for the sake of other men, and that is God's plan for human life. One man going first. One man being the spearhead of the world's advance. One man bearing the burden for his fellows. One man carrying a cross.

And if it be asked what this means for the church of our day, there is no simpler way of phrasing the answer than to say that it is the church's task to bear the necessary burden, to make the needed sacrifice, to carry the cross. For if not to Christians, to whom else can God turn?

Chapter XI

HAVE FAITH IN GOD

And Jesus answered them, "Have faith in God." Mark 11:22

IN A NATIONWIDE SURVEY SPONSORED A FEW YEARS AGO BY THE *Ladies' Home Journal* it was discovered that 95 per cent of the American people believed in God. Some of them called God "the giver of all things and our creator." Others said that he was a "spirit within the individual." Still others described him as "a force with intelligence." But whatever the words with which they identified him, 95 per cent of all the people questioned said that they believed in him.

When these same people were asked about their convictions concerning prayer, 90 per cent of them indicated that they believed in it enough to practice it, and 74 per cent said that they prayed frequently. And when the questions turned to immortality, 73 per cent of the people replied that they believed in a life which goes on beyond the grave.

At first glance the results of this survey appear to show that the faith of our fathers is also the faith of their children. They seem to prove that this is a very religious nation. "In God We Trust" we inscribe upon our coins, and it looks as if the evidence bears out the truth of the claim. Yet the mind quickly grows uneasy when we compare these brave professions of faith with certain other facts in the contemporary scene. We think, for example, about the incredible waste of life and resources in crime, vice, war, economic competition, and selfish ambition. We think about the vast companies of people who are emotionally disturbed—worried, afraid, jealous, hateful, frustrated, hopeless. "If 95 per cent of the people of this nation believe in God," we say to ourselves, "if 90 per cent of them believe in prayer, if 73 per cent believe in life eternal—how does it happen that faith makes so little difference in daily living? Why is it that we are not kinder people, calmer people, wiser people, better people?"

And thus we find ourselves confronted with three basic questions: (1) What is faith? (2) What is the *Christian* faith? and (3) How can we transform faith into life?

I

When we ask ourselves the first question—What is faith?—it is probable that there is no better answer than that given in the Letter to the Hebrews: "Faith is the assurance of things hoped for, the conviction of things not seen." The definition is quite simple, but it gives rise to several important implications.

For one thing, faith is always dealing with matters which have not been proved and perhaps cannot be proved. Faith is the assurance of things *hoped for*. It is the conviction of things *not seen*. When people speak of faith with scorn because it is not buttressed by irrefutable demonstration, they only betray their lack of knowledge with regard to the true nature of faith. If we can prove a given proposition, we do not speak of it in terms of faith but of fact. We do not say that we *believe* it: we say that we *know* it. As George Buttrick puts it:

The modern demand that we "prove" Christianity, presumably by some kind of scientific demonstration, should appall us. It is as if Columbus had sat down on the coast of Spain and refused to move until someone brought him his desired continent. . . . When people demand that Christianity be proved before they will accept it, we should perhaps reply, "Even in science the proof is found only through the experiment." [1]

[1] *Christ and Man's Dilemma* (New York and Nashville: Abingdon Press, 1946).

When faith moves in the realms of the soul, however, not even experiment can surely sustain it with proof for other people. In that area it is of faith's essence that it cannot be proved.

Moreover, having faith does not mean having no problems. As one writer suggests, faith does not mean the removal of all fear, insurance against calamity, dissociation from sorrow, the coming of utopia, or the discovery of some secret formula whereby all of our difficulties can safely be left to God while we lie back in parasitic restfulness. Men of faith are still men, and perplexing problems and baffling dilemmas are inseparable from our human creaturehood.

Robert Clairmont has written a set of four couplets which he calls "The Answers," and they have a bearing on this insight:

> "When did the world begin and how?"
> I asked a lamb, a goat, a cow:
>
> "What's it all about and why?"
> I asked a hog as he went by:
>
> "Where will the whole thing end and when?"
> I asked a duck, a goose, a hen:
>
> And I copied all the answers, too,
> A quack, a honk, an oink, a moo.[2]

No man ever lives without confronting at last a considerable assemblage of questions to which no better answers are available than these; for whatever else faith means, it does not involve having no problems.

But although religious faith deals with convictions which cannot be proved and although not even the strongest faith in the world can lift from our hearts the full load of their burdens, any faith

---

[2] Quoted in *Modern Treasury of Humorous Verse,* copyrighted 1945 by Coward-McCann, Inc.

worthy of the name is still inextricably interwoven with the soundest reasoning which the mind can devise. Faith is the *assurance* of things hoped for and the *conviction* of things not seen, and we do not have assurance about things which are unreasonable nor do we hold convictions in support of claims which seem foolish. Faith is never opposed to reason: it does not mean believing things which are not true. Faith is opposed to sight: it involves believing what you have good reason to believe but cannot absolutely prove.

It has been said that "faith is inference based upon experience, our experience or that of the race," and although it must never be forgotten that faith never escapes from the category of unprovable inference, it must never be overlooked either that faith always stands upon the sure rock of experience. For faith is always reasonable.

And then faith is an inescapable ingredient of all human living. It is not confined to religion: it has a large place in every part of man's life on the earth.

One cold October day we were driving down the Maine coast when we came to a section of the road lined with countless little cabins meant to house the transient traffic of the summer. There were no guests in any of these houses; for the summer season was past and gone. Moreover, many long months must go by before any more guests could be expected; for the next summer season was still far distant. But all around the cabins men were working. They were replacing clapboards, rebuilding steps, repointing chimneys. They were preparing. They were getting ready. And they were building on a foundation of faith of which they probably were not even aware. They did not know that summer would come again. They could not demonstrate or prove it, and the only justification of their labor was the confidence that what had happened many times before was going to happen again.

So it is in all of our living. I put my money in the bank in the faith that the banks are dependable. I step into a boat in the faith that it will float. I set down my hammer on the bench in the faith that it will stay where I put it. I buy a can of soup in the faith that since the label claims the can contains beef with noodles, I shall not open it to find mock turtle. No man can prove that his wife has been faithful to him. No woman can demonstrate beyond all doubt that her best friend is not telling other people lies about her. Whether we like it or not, we live by faith in everything we think or say or do. For faith is an inescapable ingredient of all human living.

Faith, then, is the assurance of things hoped for and the conviction of things not seen. It always deals with matters which have not been proved and perhaps cannot be proved, and it can never be approached as the answer to all of our problems. But its roots are deep sunk in the ground of our reason, and without it we could not even live.

II

Yet when all this has been said, we still have scarcely touched that way of thinking and living which we have in mind when we speak about our *Christian* faith. When we add to the noun "faith" the adjective "Christian," we define it, give it content, and make it specific. And we make it necessary to ask ourselves the second of the three questions which I posed a little while ago: What makes faith *Christian* faith?

It ought to be obvious to everyone that the Christian faith means something more than the conviction that it is not nice to be rude to elderly ladies. It should be clear to all of us that the Christian faith involves more than doing a good deed every day, accepting the Golden Rule as a wise standard of conduct, refusing to drink, gamble, steal, murder, or commit adultery. The Christian faith is best described by its own documents, and we find its essence in the affirmation that "the Word became flesh and dwelt among us," or that "God was in Christ reconciling the world to himself," or that "God so loved the world that he gave his only Son, that who-

ever believes in him should not perish but have eternal life." We find
the Christian faith in the words of Peter when he answered the
question of Jesus: "You are the Christ, the Son of the living God."
We find it in the words of Jesus himself as John reports them: "He
who has seen me has seen the Father." If we had to choose a single
biblical narrative to illustrate what we mean by the Christian faith,
it would probably be one of the stories of the Resurrection, and if we
needed a single doctrinal statement, it would doubtless be the
Trinity—the confidence that almighty and eternal God, who
created the world in the beginning and governs it still today, was
once made incarnate in the person of Jesus Christ, and through
his Holy Spirit ever dwells upon the doorstep of even the humblest
human heart.

This is the historic and unchanging faith which the church has
preached through all the years since Jesus walked the earth himself, and that faith carries with it two important meanings for all
Christian people today.

For one thing, it lays a heavy burden on the followers of Jesus. No
one of us is expected to *be* Christ, but all of us are called upon to
be *like* Christ. The followers of Jesus are meant to be just that—
followers of Jesus. The life he lived is intended to be a pattern for
our own, and the more we know about it, the more surely we find
it taking the form of a cross.

Jesus loved his enemies, did good to those who hated him, prayed
for those who despitefully used him, turned the other cheek, went
the second mile, gave himself to death that he might lead evil men
to life. "If any man would come after me," he said, "let him deny
himself and take up his cross *and follow me.*" (Italics mine.) And
that is precisely how the Christian faith becomes manifest in daily
living now. Not in peace of mind. Not in a life of physical comfort
and economic security. Not in affirmative answers to all of our
prayers. Far surer signs of the Christian faith are men who choose
their vocations from motives of service; who use their spare time

in areas helpful to their fellows; who forego their self-pampering luxuries and spend the money to feed the hungry, clothe the naked, or bring the word of Christ to those who have not heard or heeded it; who place their Christian witness in a higher category than their professional advancement, social standing, economic security, or reputation for patriotism.

A Jewish rabbi once made this comment to a Christian congregation: "Take the cross out of your religion, and we can be one." But Christians cannot take the cross out of their religion. To remove the cross from Christianity would be like removing the heart from a human body: both the heartless body and the crossless Christianity would die. For the Christian faith is inseparable from the life of self-sacrifice. It is inseparable from the cross.

But the Christian faith has a second meaning for our living today; for if it lays a heavy burden on the followers of Jesus, it also gives them what they need to carry it. "It is one of the greatest principles of Christianity," said Pascal, "that that which happened in Jesus Christ may happen in the soul of every Christian," and if the Christian faith has affinities with Calvary today, it also has a kinship with the Resurrection. For through the life and death and resurrection of his Lord the Christian finds the assurance that man is not sailing in a rudderless craft, that he is not riding in a driverless car, that the heart of the universe is sound, and that the future of the universe is safe. He finds the confidence that although evil often builds mighty bulwarks, God always tears them down. He finds the faith that although goodness often seems to speak in nothing but the still, small voice which is neither heard nor heeded, God makes of it at last a trumpet drowning out the roar of the thunder of wrong. The Christian gospel means that history is in God's hands. He can be delayed, but he cannot be defeated, and in his own good time he rolls back the stones from the doors of the man-made tombs of the world and raises from the dead the Saviors of mankind.

III

This, then, is the Christian faith. This is the faith which we claim that we possess ourselves, but if we really have it, why has it made so little difference in our lives? Why are we so similar to people who make no claim to Christian faith at all? Why are we not more joyful, confident, patient, loving, courageous, committed? And how are we to transform our faith into our lives?

One of the principal reasons for our failure is the fact that while it can be said that we have faith, it can also be said that we do not have much faith in our faith. Asked if we believed these affirmations which I have been making, most of us would probably say that we do; but when it comes actually to risking our bank accounts, our jobs, our reputations, our freedom, or our physical safety to that faith, we usually are not ready. We are like the man who tells you that the bridge across the canyon is perfectly safe but who will not walk across the bridge himself. We are like the woman who knows that she has a good strong body but who keeps reaching up to touch her head and be sure that her neck is still holding it on.

There is a sense in which our faith is operating best when it is completely ignored. We have faith, for example, that the sun will rise each morning in the east, and we best make use of that faith not by setting our alarms for four o'clock and rushing out on our lawns to prove to ourselves that our faith is justified but by acting on the faith—arranging our waking and sleeping hours in conformity with it—and forgetting it. This does not mean, of course, that a premium is to be placed upon the acceptance of the Christian faith without any rational justification. God gave us our minds and expects them to be used in our churches no less than in our schools and our businesses. A man will have to find the Christian faith reasonable, or he will never make that faith his own, and there is plenty of space in the Christian community for thinking, doubting, discussing, and debating. But the time comes at last when a man has to bet his life on something—that God exists or that he doesn't, that Christ was a true revelation of God or that he wasn't, that the Christian life is of supreme importance or that it isn't. And once it has been decided to accept the Christian faith, it is one of the requirements for using it successfully that it be treated like those many other convictions which are no longer open to serious question, like our belief in washing the face and brushing the teeth, refraining from murder and theft, and driving on the side of the road prescribed by the laws of our land.

Such faith in our faith is needed if Christianity is ever to be effective either in us or in the world at large, and the way in which it would work is not hard to discover. "If your enemy is hungry," Paul said, "feed him; if he is thirsty, give him drink." When famine struck China a few years ago, there were many to say that we should not use our bulging surpluses to feed the Chinese. After all, were not the Chinese our enemies, and where was the wisdom in adding to their war potential? But having faith in our faith, we should never raise the latter questions at all. No man is ever half so much our enemy as he is our brother. Satan can never be cast out by Satan nor evil destroyed by evil; and having faith in our faith, we would simply feed our enemy when he hungered and forget about the matter. Jesus said:

Do not be anxious, saying, "What shall we eat?" or "What shall we drink?" or "What shall we wear?" . . . But seek first [God's] kingdom and his righteousness, and all these things shall be yours as well.

For the most part, however, God's righteousness is the last thing we seek. There are so many other things we have to be sure about first —what effect a given act or decision is going to have on our pocketbook, our social standing, our professional advancement, our national security. But having faith in our faith, we should put these latter issues in a secondary position. We should try to discern God's will in the matter, and having done it, we should forget about it.

Having faith in our faith means refusing to be religious hypocrites, claiming a faith we neither possess nor dare to try; refusing to be spiritual hypochondriacs, always taking our own temperatures to make sure that our souls are still healthy; refusing to be Calamity Janes, always waiting for something bad to happen and just a little disappointed when it doesn't; refusing to be troublesome imitators of the ancient Atlas, always thinking that we have to hold up the whole world on our own shoulders.

Having faith in our faith involves what Glenn Clark calls "the capacity to let go," the putting of one's whole life utterly in the hands of God and the commitment of man's faithfulness to God's providence. It presupposes the possession of the precious quality of personal courage. It requires that Christians lose some of their concern about the immediate consequences of their actions and become more willing to trust God to know what is going to happen when people do what he asks them to do. It is another way of saying that Christians dare to be Christian in the attitudes they hold, the words they speak, the decisions they make, the deeds they do.

In A. J. Cronin's novel *The Citadel,* Andrew Manson is a young doctor in the shabby little town of Blaenelly who fights the ignorance, encourages the understanding, and helps to heal the bodies of the simple mining folk. The story concerns his marriage to Christine, the long, hard years of their struggle side by side, the crucial days when it seemed that Andrew might surrender to the temptations of a more comfortable life, and then, after the ship had been righted and was sailing on an even keel again, that terrible night when Christine dashed across the street to get Andrew some of his favorite cheese and they brought her back dead.

Some time later, as Andrew struggled to realize the dreams which

Christine had cherished for him, he went to Kensal Green and in Cronin's words he

entered the cemetery, stood a long time at Christine's grave. . . . It was a bright, fresh afternoon, with that crispness in the breeze which she had always loved. . . .

When at last he turned away, hastening for fear he should be late, there in the sky before him a bank of cloud lay brightly, bearing the shape of battlements.

That is what life presents to all of us. Battlements! And for the taking of them it is essential that we have faith in something other than ourselves. We must obey the command of Jesus: we must have faith—in God.

Chapter XII

BE PERFECT

You, therefore, must be perfect, as your heavenly Father is perfect.   Matt. 5:48

THIS STRANGE COMMAND OF JESUS BECOMES MORE COMPREHEN-sible when we hold it up beside a similar command of Paul. "Be imitators of God," Paul wrote to the Ephesians, and at first his words seem as impossible and even blasphemous as those of Jesus himself.

Yet if we were made in God's image, is it wrong that we covet God's likeness? If we are God's children, is it not a matter of tremendous consequence that we follow our Father's example? One cf the most troublesome problems of life is the separation of the good from the bad, the wise from the foolish, the true from the false. In the imitation of God there is a clear, straight road through the stormy swamps of our spiritual blindness in the choices we must make and through our sense of futility as our good intentions seem so often to do no more than serve the purposes which we despise; and is it not a sign of wisdom when we take that road?

It is in this sense that these words of Jesus are to be understood. Not that any one of us is expected to be perfect in the sense of being flawless. Not that following Jesus is inseparably linked with a perfection so obviously unattainable that following Jesus becomes impossible too. Instead, we are to be perfect in the sense that we aim at perfection, that we judge our lives in terms of him who alone is perfect, that we imitate God in all we think and say and do.

And how many attributes of God there are which open avenues

on which the faithful follower of Jesus can obey his command to be perfect as our heavenly Father is perfect.

I

Think first about the diligence of God. When his enemies attacked him for healing a man on the Sabbath day, Jesus replied simply, "My Father is working still, and I am working." That insight is sound, and it is a humbling recollection that through all of the unimaginable ages of God's existence, God has been a laborer.

Year after year God brings to pass in constant faithfulness the day for sowing and the time for reaping. Day by day, hour by hour, and minute by minute he gives life to the seed and food to the flowers, the grass, and the trees. Let a man and woman decide to add a baby to their home, and in the mother's womb God works to shape the embryo to human life and give it eyes and arms and legs. When a body is wounded, God starts at once to stay the flow of blood and halt the infection, and when a man or animal is ill, God sends his healing power coursing through the arteries and veins. The appearance of evil is the signal for God to oppose it, and no man fights for righteousness without God's strength and love beside him.

There is no meaningful imitation of God's perfection which does not include the imitation of his diligence in labor and toil. To be like God in such diligence requires that we avoid the laziness which drove an overworked wife to say about her recently deceased husband: "I'll get some work out of that old boy yet. I'll have him cremated and put his ashes in an hourglass!" To be like God in diligence requires not simply that we be working but also that we be working for the right causes and that we make for our own lives such a decision as was made by the tavern owner in Texas who piled his stock of brew on the sidewalk in front of his store and announced as he walked away from it, "I decided to stop working for the Devil and go to work for the Lord."

But most important of all, being like God in his diligence involves realizing that worthy life *is* labor, that creation is always hard, and that the right and the good never happen by chance but always come into being because someone has worked to give them life. Honest government, healthy children, adequate schools, peace among the nations, food for the starving, shelter for the homeless—these fruits do not grow except upon the trees of faithful work performed in our homes, churches, school committees, relief agencies, and town and city offices. "You, therefore, must be perfect, as your heavenly Father is perfect," Jesus said and we cannot follow his counsel today unless we first imitate God's diligence.

II

In the second place, think about the impartiality of God. On a cool summer morning in Maine my wife and I had gone out with a lobster fisherman to watch him haul his traps, and while he ate his lunch at noon he told us about a terrible northeast storm which had swept down the coast a few winters ago. One of the little fishing boats was lost at sea, and as the night came on and the snow closed in, even the Coast Guard vessels were compelled to return from the search. The three men on the boat were dead, they told the watchers on the island shore. No one could be out in that storm and survive.

But far out on the ocean the three men were still living. When it became obvious that they could not get back to the harbor in the gale, they had dropped their heavy anchor and settled down to weather it out. About midnight the storm abated a little, and through the wildly swirling flakes of snow they caught sight of the light on Baker's Island. To lessen the strain on the anchor they had been forced to keep their engine running continuously, and with the gasoline fast disappearing, they felt that they had no choice but to run for port. So they tied a rope around one of the men and sent him forward to pull up the anchor, and to make the work a little easier the pilot sent the boat forward to loosen the tension on the chain. But just then a sudden surge of the waves brought the chain taut, and it parted; and as the boat swung around broadside, a great sea crashed into the cockpit and completely flooded it. At two o'clock the next morning the boat limped into the harbor, and later in the day the Coast Guard officers came out to the island to check the foolish rumor that the men were actually alive. It was not possible, they said.

And then the fisherman who was telling us the story asked if we knew what he had told his wife as he stood on the shore. "I told her," he said, "that next Sunday she could go to church alone. The fellow who ran that boat is an atheist. He doesn't believe in God, and he never goes to church. But God had a hand in bringing in that boat, and I told my wife that if that was what God did for people who paid no attention to him, she could go to church by herself. I was through with it!"

For the first time in his life, apparently, that fisherman had come face to face with the stark impartiality of God. For the first time in his life he was wrestling with the problem which Jesus stated when he said that God "makes his sun rise on the evil and on the good, and sends rain on the just and on the unjust." And he did not yet understand that if we want to be sons of our Father in heaven, we must also be like him in this.

God treats everyone alike. His goodness is never conditional upon the merit of the people to whom he is good, and if he has no choice but pain for humankind, he lays its risks or burdens equally on all. An automobile will operate equally effectively for the man who is using it to rob a bank and for the man who is using it to carry his sick wife to the hospital. Cancer strikes down the dope peddler who seeks nothing but his own enrichment, but it also strikes down the young mother who longs only to bring up her children in the love of the Lord. Food nourishes the saint, but it nourishes the sinner too. And when a hurricane roars down on a

120

city, the homes of the righteous are no more frequently spared than the homes of the wicked.

That there is mystery in this impartiality of God no man will deny, and the existence of evil is a problem which men on earth will doubtless never fully solve. But this at least we know: God does not have two faces, and if we seek to be like him, we, too, must have one countenance to show to all our fellows—one mind, one heart, one will. Honest or dishonest, kind or cruel, lovely or ugly, friend or foe—each man must find in us the same, unchanging desire to understand him, to love him, and to give support to any striving which he makes to be the kind of person God intended him to be. God "makes his sun rise on the evil and on the good, and sends rain on the just and on the unjust." If we would be sons of our Father in heaven, we cannot do otherwise than imitate this holy impartiality by which God refuses to say that while one man is worthy of his love, another man is not, or that while it is justifiable that one man run the common risks of earthly life, another should be spared.

III

And then, third, consider the quietness of God. We often wish that God might be more in evidence around us. When Hitler sent his armies crashing east and west, the Christian world might deplore his ruthlessness, but it could not deny his existence. When the bomb was dropped on Hiroshima, the Japanese might question our humanity, but they could not doubt our military power. And so, on an immeasurably higher plane, we should like to have it be with God. A robber holds up a bank, and why does not God wrest the gun from his hand and drag him off to the police station? An airliner speeds through the night toward a high mountain crag, and why does not God heave the plane upward in time to save the lives of the twenty-five young soldiers going home for Christmas? The Russians keep the world in turmoil, and why does not God blow up the Kremlin?

But whether we like it or not, God does not work in that way, and the ancient story of Elijah on the mountain speaks of truth much needed among us:

And behold, the Lord passed by, and a great and strong wind rent the mountains, and broke in pieces the rocks before the Lord, but the Lord was not in the wind; and after the wind an earthquake, but the Lord was not in the earthquake; and after the earthquake a fire, but the Lord was not in the fire; and after the fire a still small voice.

The point is not that God had no connection with the earthquake, the wind, and the fire; for they did not happen until "the Lord passed by." The point is rather that the earthquake, the wind, and the fire were only incidental manifestations of the still small voice. They were the sound of God's footsteps, the aftermath of God's presence, the result of God's passing. But God himself was not in them: He was in the quietness of the still small voice.

It seems to be true that God keeps off the stage as much as possible, that he uses persuasion more frequently than force, and that he whispers more often than he shouts. The wondrous gift is given silently. The needed word is spoken quietly. The helping hand is offered unobtrusively.

And the true sons of the heavenly Father are like him in his quietness. They have no kinship with the demagogue, no hunger to be paraded, no joy in pomp and circumstance. They are more concerned about being than seeming, more eager to give than to be known as the giver. In the midst of the changing they have fastened their lives to the changeless. Their roots strike deep enough to hold them erect but not unbending, and not needing to be praised, they are not frightened to be taken for granted. They rejoice in righteousness and find its victory no sweeter when they themselves have been its herald than when the world stamps other names upon it. They have more hope in education than in legislation, hold more faith in mercy than in retribution, put more trust in love than in compulsion. For they have learned that if they would bear upon themselves the likeness of their Father, they cannot repudiate the quietness which is inseparable from him.

IV

Finally, remember the patience of God. How long man has lived on earth we do not know, nor can we say when the earth itself came into being, nor could we even hazard a guess about how many aeons earlier the universe began. But against the total span of universal time the life of man on earth is seen as just starting, and suddenly we realize that man's coming to the earth required preparation extending over ages untold and ever untellable.

Moreover, when we turn to the five thousand years or more of man's actually recorded history, we find that the patience of God in preparing for man is as nothing in comparison with his patience in dealing with man. Think of the civilizations which have come to the earth and departed. Recall the nations begotten and destroyed. Imagine the millions upon millions of individual men and women whose birth, life, and death have been a part of earth's experience. How many times God has shown his people that a culture standing on oppression will not long stand! How many times God has made it clear that war destroys not only the victim but also the victor! How many times God has given men the chance to learn that he has made of one blood all the peoples of the earth, that the sexual relationship becomes intolerable when its justification is lust and not love, that the self-seeking life is the self-destroying life, that whatsoever a man sows he also reaps, that man is not the owner of the world but only its steward!

Have you never marveled at God's incredible endurance of man's blindness and arrogance? Have you never wondered why God did not rise up in fury, destroy man altogether, and put an end to the whole sorry mess? When we read that Jesus told Peter to forgive his brother not simply seven times but "seventy times seven," we often think such patience foolish, but this is just what God has been doing for uncounted millions of years with uncounted millions of people—teaching, persuading, pleading, hoping, forgiving. The humility of God is past man's understanding. The patience of God exceeds our comprehension.

Yet there is no significant attempt to be perfect as our heavenly Father is perfect which does not include being patient as he himself is patient. Impatience is a form of blasphemy. It is the denial of God's wisdom or God's power or God's love. It indicates the belief that God does not know what he is doing, or that the universe is out of God's control, or that we cannot depend on God to be good.

Walt Kelly has a provocative sequence of drawings in which Pogo is resting one day beside a fallen log when suddenly the rabbit rushes past. "Whoosh! Whoosh! Whoosh!" the rabbit pants, and when Pogo asks him where he is going, he replies that he does not know but that he is hurrying off to meet an emergency. "What's all the hurry if you don't know where?" Pogo inquires, and the rabbit answers, "Man! That's jes' it! It's when you don't know where you is goin' that you gotta be in a hurry!"

The sons of the Father find the strength to be patient as the Father is patient because they know not only where they are going but also where they are and whence they came. They came from God in the beginning. In God they live and move and have their being now. And day by day they surge forward into a fullness of living and serving which has no end in time or space. Because they have forever, they have no need for haste, and because they build for the ages, they cannot tolerate the carelessness of the camper who builds his lean-to only for the night.

So the true sons of the Father are content to spend twenty years of their lives in bringing the child in their home to the fullness of wisdom and strength. When a long-cherished dream is destroyed, they do not eat their souls away in bitterness but clear the rubble and rear again the walls which crumbled. If peace cannot come in their own time, they are satisfied to work for its coming in someone else's time. Frustrated, they transform their failure into food for inner growth. Interrupted, they make the interruption an opportunity for insight and service far beyond the labor interrupted. In the days of Noah, Peter said, "God's patience waited." It still does, and in the imitation of the God who bears all things and endures all things the constancy of calm persistence occupies a large and unavoidable place.

The diligence of God, the impartiality of God, the quietness of God, the patience of God—how few these are among the attributes of the heavenly Father which Paul must have had in mind when he counseled men to be God's imitators. Add his justice, color blindness, forgiveness, and love, and even then you have scarcely begun to describe the wonder of his being and the incredible complexity of any attempt to be like him.

Yet still the commandment of Jesus is incumbent upon us. "You . . . must be perfect," he said, "as your heavenly Father is perfect" —perfect not in the sense of having no faults but perfect rather in the sense that we share God's purposes, respond to his will, feed on his goodness, walk in his light. "The godly man has perished from the earth," Micah said. God have mercy on us if he has! For with the godly man, who finds in his heavenly Father the life toward which he himself strives, rests God's last hope for mankind on the earth.